English for Socializing and Small Talk

Sylee Gore and David Gordon Smith

SHORT COURSE SERIES

Verfasser	Sylee Gore, Berlin; David Gordon Smith, Berlin
Kritische Durchsicht	Marion Grussendorf, Köln; Louise Kennedy, Hamburg
Außenredaktion	Christine House
Verlagsredaktion	Janan Barksdale, Susanne Schütz
Redaktionelle Mitarbeit	Oliver Busch, Dr. Sabine Krämer, Gabriela Lund (Wortliste), Kari-ann Seamark
Bildredaktion	Elizabeth Hine, Uta Hübner
Gesamtgestaltung und technische Umsetzung	Sylvia Lang
Bildquellen	*Titelfoto:* FontShop, Berlin *Cartoons & Illustrationen:* Oxford Designers & Illustrators *Symbole:* Andreas Terglane, Kassel *Fotos:* C.Buckstegen: S.14, 20, 23, 27, 41, 43, 46; Corbis GmbH: S. 5/RF, 48/D.Katzenstein, 50/K.Dodge, 55/RF; Getty Images: S. 7/China Tourism Press, 11/RF, 26/B. Handelman, 34/B.Winebrenner, 38/RF, 44/ B. Erlanson, 48/RF (2), 52/S.Peters, 57/RF; FontShop: S.5 (4), 8, 13, 14, 17, 22 (4), 23, 31, 39, 40, 48, 49, 59
Tonaufnahmen	*Aufnahmestudio:* The Audio Workshop, London *Aufnahmeleitung:* Andrew Branch, RBA Productions *Toningenieur:* Joseph Degnan *Sprecher:* Brian Bowles, Lynne Brackley, James Goode, Eve Karpf, Steven Pacey

Herzlichen Dank für die Unterstützung an: Günther Becker, Matthias Fuchs, Marco Lawrenz, Marit Reifenstein, Jürgen Schmidt, Nicolas Sconza, Sarah Smith, Stefan Winthe

Weitere Titel in der *Short Course Series*:

English for Accounting	ISBN-13: 978-3-464-01880-4;	ISBN-10: 3-464-01880-6
English for the Automobile Industry	ISBN-13: 978-3-464-01877-4;	ISBN-10: 3-464-01877-6
English for Customer Care	ISBN-13: 978-3-464-01882-8;	ISBN-10: 3-464-01882-2
English for Emails	ISBN-13: 978-3-464-01878-1;	ISBN-10: 3-464-01878-4
English for Human Resources	ISBN-13: 978-3-464-01881-1;	ISBN-10: 3-464-01881-4
English for Marketing and Advertising	ISBN-13: 978-3-464-01876-7	ISBN-10: 3-464-01876-8
English for Meetings	ISBN-13: 978-3-464-01874-3;	ISBN-10: 3-464-01874-1
English for Presentations	ISBN-13: 978-3-464-01875-0;	ISBN-10: 3-464-01875-X
English for Telephoning	ISBN-13: 978-3-464-01873-6;	ISBN-10: 3-464-01873-3

www.cornelsen.de

Die Internetadressen und -dateien, die in diesem Lehrwerk angegeben sind, wurden vor Drucklegung geprüft. Der Verlag übernimmt keine Gewähr für die Aktualität und den Inhalt dieser Adressen und Dateien oder solcher, die mit ihnen verlinkt sind.

1. Auflage, 1. Druck 2006

Alle Drucke dieser Auflage sind inhaltlich unverändert und können im Unterricht nebeneinander verwendet werden.

© 2006 Cornelsen Verlag, Berlin

Das Werk und seine Teile sind urheberrechtlich geschützt. Jede Nutzung in anderen als den gesetzlich zugelassenen Fällen bedarf der vorherigen schriftlichen Einwilligung des Verlages. Hinweis zu § 52 a UrhG: Weder das Werk noch seine Teile dürfen ohne eine solche Einwilligung eingescannt und in ein Netzwerk eingestellt werden. Dies gilt auch für Intranets von Schulen und sonstigen Bildungseinrichtungen.

Druck: CS-Druck CornelsenStürtz, Berlin

ISBN-13: 978-3-464-20156-5
ISBN-10: 3-464-20156-2

 Inhalt gedruckt auf säurefreiem Papier aus nachhaltiger Forstwirtschaft.

Inhalt

PAGE	TITLE	TOPICS	LANGUAGE TIPS AND STRATEGIES
5	**1 Making contact**	Making arrangements via email Meeting visitors on arrival Talking about the weather Talking about plans	Attitudes to time in different cultures Talking about the future
14	**2 Welcoming visitors**	Welcoming visitors to your company Talking about the offices and the company Offering a visitor refreshments Giving directions in a building Introducing a visitor	Using first names Asking for clarification
23	**3 Getting acquainted**	Making small talk before a meeting Talking about personal possessions Talking about free-time activities Talking about travel and places you have visited Following up a visit with an email	Moving from small talk to business Talking about mutual acquaintances Keeping a conversation going
31	**4 Entertaining a visitor**	Showing a visitor around your town Talking about the place where you live Recommending things to do and places to see Giving directions in a town or city	Talking about recent German history 'Used to' Talking about origins Dealing with invitations
40	**5 Eating out**	Making small talk in a restaurant Deciding what to order Talking about family and relationships Talking about education Thanking somebody for a meal	Explaining a menu Commenting on what someone says 'Seriously' – the role of humour in different cultures
49	**6 Networking at a trade fair**	Starting a conversation with a stranger Talking about your company Talking about products at the stand Trying out new small-talk topics Following up a new contact via email	Networking tips Safe small-talk topics Ending a conversation politely Telling a story or an anecdote

PAGE	APPENDIX
58	**Test yourself!**
60	**Partner files Partner A**
62	**Partner files Partner B**
64	**Answer key**
69	**Transcripts**
75	**A–Z word list**
78	**Useful phrases and vocabulary**
83	**Vocabulary banks**

Vorwort

English for Socializing and Small Talk richtet sich an alle, die sicher auf ausländische Geschäftspartner zugehen und vertrauensvolle Kontakte mit ihnen aufbauen wollen. Ob bei einem Geschäftsessen, ob an einem Messestand, ob Sie einen ausländischen Besucher durch Ihr Unternehmen führen oder mit ihm am Ende eines Arbeitstages gemeinsam eine Freizeitveranstaltung besuchen: Wer erfolgreich Geschäftsbeziehungen aufbauen und pflegen möchte, muss sich sprachlich sicher und angemessen bewegen können. **English for Socializing and Small Talk** vermittelt Ihnen alle sprachlichen Strukturen und Redewendungen, die Sie benötigen, um erfolgreich auf Englisch Konversation zu betreiben und Kontakte zu knüpfen und auszubauen.

In den sechs Units von **English for Socializing and Small Talk** werden typische Situationen dargestellt, die für den Aufbau und die Pflege einer Geschäftsbeziehung wichtig sind. Eine ganze Reihe gut strukturierter, abwechslungsreicher und interessanter Übungen und Aktivitäten erlauben Ihnen, die Redemittel und Strategien gezielt einzuüben. Auf der beiliegenden **Audio CD** findet sich eine Vielzahl realistischer Dialoge, in denen die sprachlichen Mittel im Kontext präsentiert werden. Speziell die **Partner Files** im Anhang, auf die in den Units jeweils verwiesen wird, bieten Übungen in Form von Rollenspielen, die es Ihnen ermöglichen, den erlernten Wortschatz mit einem Partner oder einer Partnerin zu trainieren. Darüber hinaus werden in **English for Socializing and Small Talk** auch interkulturelle Aspekte und Soft Skills besprochen

Jede Unit beginnt mit **Breaking the ice**, dem Einstieg in das Thema der jeweiligen Lektion. Hier finden Sie Aktivitäten, die zum Sprechen anregen. Auch sensibilisieren diese Aufgaben Sie für mögliche Schwierigkeiten, die auftreten können, wenn Sie im Umgang mit Geschäftspartnern eine angenehme Atmosphäre aufbauen, Höflichkeiten austauschen oder einfach ungezwungen plaudern wollen. Den abschließenden Teil einer Unit bildet das **Wrapping up**. Dies sind Lesetexte, die das Thema der Lektion vertiefen oder weitere nützliche Tipps enthalten und ihrerseits zum Diskutieren anregen. Wenn alle Units bearbeitet sind, lädt Sie ein Kreuzworträtsel **Test yourself!** ein, Ihren Kenntnisstand zu überprüfen – und das in einer Form, die Spaß macht.

English for Socializing and Small Talk ist auch als Selbstlernmaterial geeignet. Es gibt einen **Answer key**, so dass Sie Ihre Antworten zu den Übungen eigenständig überprüfen können. Im Anhang befindet sich außerdem neben der **A–Z word list** eine praktische Zusammenstellung aller **Useful phrases**, die Sie kennen sollten, wenn Sie auf Englisch Konversation betreiben oder Geschäftspartner unterhalten möchten. Hier finden Sie auch viele Redewendungen und den Wortschatz, der zum Sprechen über weit verbreitete Small Talk-Themen nützlich sind.

Wenn Sie das Buch durchgearbeitet haben, sind Ihnen alle sprachlichen Mittel und Strategien begegnet, die Ihnen erlauben, sich auf Englisch in Small Talk-Situationen zu behaupten und Gäste angemessen zu betreuen. Unangenehmes Schweigen im Fahrstuhl oder während eines Geschäftsessens gehören der Vergangenheit an: Sie sind für jede Situation gerüstet!

1 Getting in touch

Breaking the ice

First look at some of the activities involved in socializing. Can you add anything?

- making small talk at a meeting
- greeting a visitor
- taking a visitor out to lunch or dinner
- introducing visitors
- chatting during a coffee break
- showing a visitor around your town or city
- networking at a trade fair or conference

Now work with a partner to ask and answer the following questions.

1. When and where do you need to socialize in English?
2. Who do you speak to? Are they native speakers or non-native speakers? Who do you find easier to understand?
3. What topics do you talk about? What topics are 'taboo' in your culture?
4. What do you find difficult about socializing in English? What do you enjoy?

1 Emails are often used to make arrangements for company visits. Look at the three emails below. Which email is the most formal? How can you tell?

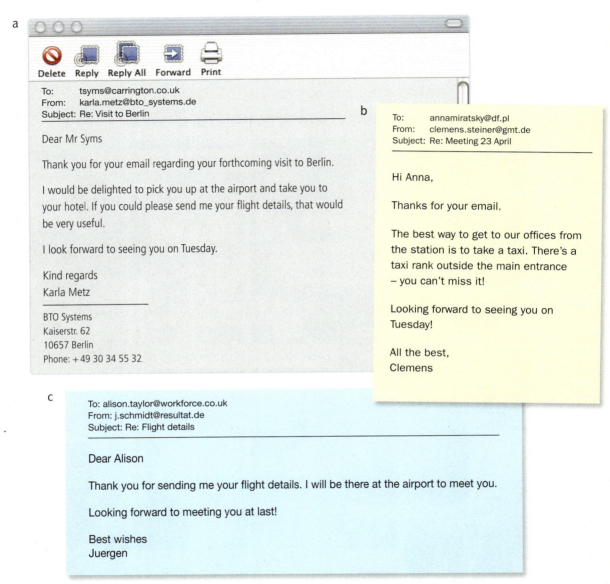

a
To: tsyms@carrington.co.uk
From: karla.metz@bto_systems.de
Subject: Re: Visit to Berlin

Dear Mr Syms

Thank you for your email regarding your forthcoming visit to Berlin.

I would be delighted to pick you up at the airport and take you to your hotel. If you could please send me your flight details, that would be very useful.

I look forward to seeing you on Tuesday.

Kind regards
Karla Metz

BTO Systems
Kaiserstr. 62
10657 Berlin
Phone: +49 30 34 55 32

b
To: annamiratsky@df.pl
From: clemens.steiner@gmt.de
Subject: Re: Meeting 23 April

Hi Anna,

Thanks for your email.

The best way to get to our offices from the station is to take a taxi. There's a taxi rank outside the main entrance – you can't miss it!

Looking forward to seeing you on Tuesday!

All the best,
Clemens

c
To: alison.taylor@workforce.co.uk
From: j.schmidt@resultat.de
Subject: Re: Flight details

Dear Alison

Thank you for sending me your flight details. I will be there at the airport to meet you.

Looking forward to meeting you at last!

Best wishes
Juergen

2 You will hear three conversations about people meeting visitors. First match the conversations to the emails above.

Conversation	Email
1	☐
2	☐
3	☐

VOCABULARY ASSISTANT
exit row seat *Sitz am Notausgang*
legroom *Beinfreiheit*
ring road *Umgehungsstraße*
uneventful *ohne Zwischenfall*

Now listen again and complete the following chart.

	Conversation 1	Conversation 2	Conversation 3
1 Have the speakers met before?			
2 Is the conversation formal or informal?			
3 Where are they meeting?			
4 What problems did the visitors have during the journey?			
5 What are they doing next?			

3 Complete the following sentences from the dialogues. Listen again if necessary.

1 You _____ be Jürgen.

2 It's great to _____ meet you in _____ after all our phone calls and emails.

3 I _____ you haven't been _____ long.

4 It's a _____ to meet you.

5 How was your _____?

6 Hi, Clemens, good to _____ you _____.

7 Sorry to keep you _____.

8 Can I _____ you with your _____?

9 Would you _____ taking this?

Which sentences above are used to …

a welcome or greet the visitor? _____

b talk about the journey? _____

c offer (or accept) help with something? _____

d apologize for a delay? _____

ATTITUDES TO TIME

Note how both Alison and Anna apologize for being late. Different cultures have different attitudes to time, meaning that what counts as 'late' varies from country to country. In Britain and the US you can usually arrive up to 15 minutes after the agreed time without being 'late'. In other countries, such as Portugal, up to 40 minutes after the agreed time is often acceptable.
What is the attitude in your country? What is considered 'late' for a business meeting or a dinner appointment?

4 Match the questions to the answers. Some questions have more than one answer.

1. Can I help you with your bags?
2. Would you mind taking this?
3. How was your flight?
4. How was your journey?
5. How was the drive?
6. Is there a toilet around here?
7. Is there a café where we could sit down?
8. Where are we going from here?

a Fine, thanks.
b I thought we could go to the hotel first.
c Long!
d Not so good. The traffic was horrible.
e Sure, no problem.
f That would be great, thanks.
g There's one just this way.
h Uneventful, thanks.
i We should probably go straight to the office, if that's OK.
j Yes, there's a nice one just over there.
k OK, but there was some turbulence.

TOILET OR RESTROOM?

British people talk about the 'toilet' *(Toilette)* or 'loo' *(Klo)*, which is more informal. 'WC' ['dʌblju: ˌsi:] is now old-fashioned.
Using the word 'toilet' is not polite in American English, however! When talking to Americans, say 'restroom' or 'bathroom'.

5 **Work with a partner to practise meeting visitors. Look at the notes in your file and try to use phrases from the box below.**

PARTNER FILES → Partner A File 1, p. 60
Partner B File 1, p. 62

MEETING VISITORS ON ARRIVAL

Greetings
Nice/Good/Great to see you again.
  (when you know sb already)
Nice/Good/Great to meet you (at last).
  (when you're meeting sb for the first time)

Apologizing for a delay
I hope you haven't been waiting long.
Sorry to keep you waiting.

Asking about the journey
How was the/your flight/journey?
How was the drive? (AE) *(if sb comes by car)*

Offering and asking for help
Can I help you with your bags?
Let me get/take that for you.
Would you mind taking this?

The next step
I'd just like to wash my hands.
Is there a toilet (BE)/restroom (AE) around here?
Is there a café where we could sit down/get something to drink?
Where are we going now?

Try to avoid these common mistakes:
~~Nice to meet you again.~~   Nice to **see** you again.
~~How was your fly?~~   How was your **flight**? (fly = *Fliege*!)
~~I take you to your hotel.~~   **I'll** take you to your hotel.

6 **Karla Metz is accompanying Mr Syms from the airport to his hotel. Look at the dialogue below and try to complete the gaps. What is the topic of their conversation?**

Mr Syms	I can't believe it's so *s*_____ ¹ here. It makes a nice change from England!
Ms Metz	How was the *w*_____ ² when you left?
Mr Syms	It was *r*_____ ³, as usual! This summer has been *t*_____ ⁴.
Ms Metz	Well, we've been very *l*_____ ⁵ here. The last couple of weeks have been very *w*_____ ⁶.
Mr Syms	Do you normally get good summers here?
Ms Metz	It depends. Usually we get at least a few *h*_____ ⁷ days, but sometimes it rains a lot.
Mr Syms	I imagine the winters here must be pretty *c*_____ ⁸.
Ms Metz	Oh yes. Sometimes it goes *d*_____ ⁹ to minus 15.
Mr Syms	Well, at least it never gets that cold in England. The winter there is usually just grey and *w*_____ ¹⁰. It can be quite depressing!
Ms Metz	Ugh! Well, I'm glad the weather is nice for your visit here …

Listen to the conversation and check your answers.

7 The 'weather' is one of the most popular small-talk topics. After all, it's a topic everybody can talk about. Put the words below into the right categories.

cloudy • cold • damp • drizzling • freezing • grey • hazy • humid • mild • overcast • pouring • rainy • roasting • sunny • warm

words describing temperature	words describing the sky	words to do with water
cold	cloudy	damp

Now use words from the table to complete these sentences.

It's _____ today.

It was _____ yesterday morning.

It was _____ yesterday evening.

The weather during my last business trip (or holiday) was _____ .

8 Mr Syms and Ms Metz are talking about their plans. Listen and complete Ms Metz's diary.

12 AUGUST

9	
10	
11	11:40 Mr Syms arrives at Tegel airport, flight BA120
12	12 (approx) _____ – Il Casolare
1	
2	
3	
4	
5	
6	
7	

9 Listen again and complete the sentences from the dialogue.

1 It's _____ now. We'll be _____ in five minutes.
2 I thought you might like to _____ your hotel first and _____ your things.
3 Then we _____ a spot of lunch. There's a nice Italian place _____ your hotel.
4 After that we _____ to the office.
5 We _____ with the sales team at 2, as you know.
6 At 4 we _____ the production plant.
7 That _____ an hour.
8 Then perhaps you _____ a taxi back to your hotel and _____ for a bit.
9 I _____ again at about 7 for dinner.
10 It _____ really good. We _____ to this fantastic Eritrean restaurant.

TALKING ABOUT PLANS

There are many ways to talk about future plans in English, and often you can say the same thing in different ways. Here are some ways to talk about plans:

- using modals verbs such as 'can', 'could', 'might', 'should', etc:
  I thought you might like to check into your hotel first.
  Then we can go to the office.
  That should only take an hour.

- using the present tense:
  We have the meeting with the sales team at 2.
  It's the big company dinner tonight.

- using 'will':
  I'll pick you up again at about 7 for dinner.

- using 'going to':
  At 4 we're going to visit the production plant.
  After that we're going to this fantastic Eritrean restaurant.

10 Work with a partner to make a dialogue. Person A: you are the host. You are dropping B off at his/her hotel. Person B: you are the visitor.

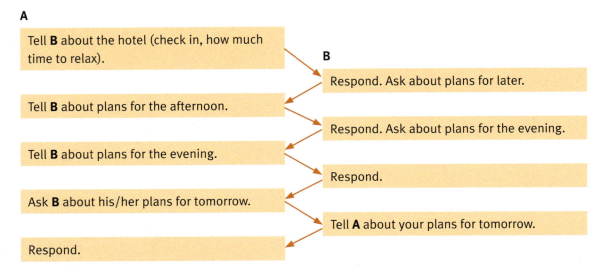

11 Complete the crossword. Then rearrange the letters in the orange squares to find the mystery phrase.

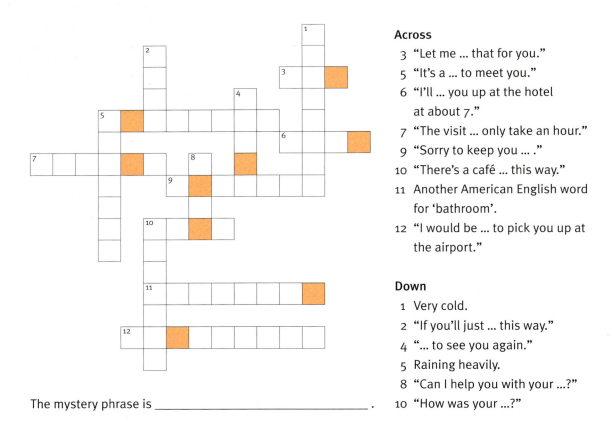

Across
3 "Let me … that for you."
5 "It's a … to meet you."
6 "I'll … you up at the hotel at about 7."
7 "The visit … only take an hour."
9 "Sorry to keep you … ."
10 "There's a café … this way."
11 Another American English word for 'bathroom'.
12 "I would be … to pick you up at the airport."

Down
1 Very cold.
2 "If you'll just … this way."
4 "… to see you again."
5 Raining heavily.
8 "Can I help you with your …?"
10 "How was your …?"

The mystery phrase is _____ .

Wrapping up

Read the article and discuss the questions which follow.

Why it's important to mix business with pleasure

Sarah Smith

Socializing with your business contacts isn't just for fun – it can also make doing business a lot easier. How many business deals have been closed not in the boardroom but in a restaurant or bar? Not everybody agrees with this, though. We look at some of the most common myths about socializing.

Myth #1: "I don't need to socialize with my business contacts."

You work long hours in the office and work hard all day long. You don't need to go to dinner with your business contacts as well, right? Wrong!

Ever since people first began trading and making deals, there has never been business without socializing. In many cultures the socializing *is* the business – people only do business with their friends, and if you're not friends already you have to become friends before you can make a deal. Even in the more 'business-like' West, socializing is still extremely important. In fact, in some countries, such as Britain, *not* socializing with business contacts is seen as very impolite and could damage your relationship.

Myth #2: "Small talk is superficial."

Many people find typical British and American small-talk topics, like the weather or sport, very superficial. Well, maybe saying it's a nice day isn't as deep as discussing Hegel or Marx. But that's not the point. This kind of small talk is a social ritual known as 'phatic' communication, where what's important is not what you say, but the fact you are talking to a particular person and keeping that relationship going.

Also, small talk doesn't always have to be about the weather, but you need to start somewhere! Building a relationship takes time. 'Superficial' small-talk topics give you a chance to start a conversation with someone. If it goes well, you can talk about 'deeper' things later.

Myth #3: "When British and American people ask 'how are you?' they don't mean it."

Yes and no. It's true that when most native speakers ask someone 'how are you?' they expect to hear an answer like 'fine, thanks' or 'not bad'. They don't really want to hear about your problems and will be surprised (and even embarrassed) if you start talking about how you really feel.

However, saying that you're fine even if you're not, doesn't need to be a bad thing. Do you really want to tell everyone you meet about your back problem or the fact that your husband has just lost his job?

But sometimes 'how are you?' can also be a real question requiring a real answer. If you're talking to someone you know well, you can tell them the truth when they ask how you are, even if you're not feeling so good. After all, talking about problems honestly can be a good way to build a relationship.

Myth #4: "English speakers behave like they're your friend, but they're not."

In the UK and the US, it's important to behave as if everyone is your friend. But this doesn't mean they're insincere. What's important is to read between the lines. Is the person just being polite, or do they really mean it? If someone says 'Let's meet up next time you're in London', they are probably just being polite. But if they give you their phone number and tell you to call them, then they really mean it. Remember: sometimes people are nice to you because they like you!

Over to you

- What are your experiences with socializing with people from other cultures? What differences (and similarities) have you experienced?
- How important is it to tell the truth in social situations?
- In what ways do you try to build a relationship with a new business contact?

Welcoming visitors

Breaking the ice

Complete the quiz below on company visitors.

When welcoming a visitor to your company, how important is it to ...

	very important	somewhat important	not important	it depends
→ find out about your visitor's company?	☐	☐	☐	☐
→ find out about your visitor's country and culture?	☐	☐	☐	☐
→ be at the reception when your visitor arrives?	☐	☐	☐	☐
→ make sure the receptionist knows how to pronounce your visitor's name?	☐	☐	☐	☐
→ give your visitor a tour of the office?	☐	☐	☐	☐
→ introduce your visitor to other members of the team?	☐	☐	☐	☐
→ offer your visitor something to eat and drink?	☐	☐	☐	☐
→ show your visitor where the toilets are?	☐	☐	☐	☐

Now discuss your answers with a partner. How often do people visit your company? Where are your visitors from? What difficulties do you have socializing with visitors to your company?

1 **Lothar Jensburg is meeting a visitor. Listen to the conversation and tick the topics they talk about.**

- the journey ☐
- the weather ☐
- the hotel ☐
- sport ☐
- the offices ☐
- the company ☐

Now listen again and answer these questions.

1 What is the visitor's name? _____
2 Have the two men met before? _____
3 Why does Lothar take the visitor into his office? _____
4 How long has the company been in its current location? _____
5 What does the visitor like about the building? _____
6 When was Vierling Design founded? _____
7 How many people work at the company? _____
8 What does the visitor want to drink? _____

> **USING FIRST NAMES**
>
> In general, Britons and Americans prefer to use first names rather than surnames. Colleagues, in particular, nearly always use first names with each other. One exception, however, is when someone of 'low status' is talking to someone of 'high status'. For example, a secretary might call the company CEO 'Ms Phillips' and the CEO would call the secretary 'Mary'.
>
> If you are not sure which name to use, then use the surname. Normally the native speaker will suggest you change to first names ("Please, call me Geoff."). Of course, *you* can also suggest it, especially if you are older or senior in position.
>
> Note that if you are using surnames, the accepted form for addressing women is 'Ms' (pronounced 'Miz'). Always use this form unless a woman says she prefers 'Mrs'. 'Miss' is hardly ever used now and sounds very old-fashioned.

2 Put the following words into the correct order to make sentences from the conversation. If necessary, listen again to check your answers.

1 trouble / us / you / did / any / have / finding / ?

   _____

2 website / clear / the / on your / very / were / directions / .

   _____

3 your briefcase and coat / leave / my office / can / you / in / .

   _____

4 to meet / round / a few members / you / take / team / of the / I'll / .

   _____

5 drink / you / to / like / would / something / ?

   _____

6 a / of / would / great / coffee / cup / be / .

   _____

3 Talking about your host's company is a good way to break the ice. Put the words below into the right categories.

> department • employees • to expand • (ground/first/second) floor •
> to be founded • hierarchy • lift • location • to move into • neighbourhood •
> reception • to restructure • staff • stairs

talking about the building	talking about the company and its history
(ground/first/second) floor	department

Use the correct form of some of the words from the table to complete these mini-dialogues.

Have you been in this _____¹ long?

No, we actually just _____² this building six months ago. It's a great _____³ – lots of green space and some nice cafés nearby.

How many people are in your company now?

How long has your company been around?

It was _____⁴ in 1972.

There are currently around 150 _____⁵. We have _____⁶ a lot in the last two years.

Which _____⁷ is your office on?

The fifth! Don't worry – we'll take the _____⁸.

Now answer the questions so they are true for you.

UNIT **2** Welcoming visitors | **17**

4 **Kathrin Oberle is visiting a company in London. Complete her parts of the dialogue with the sentences (a–g) below. Then listen to check your answers.**

a Thanks so much for arranging that.
b And the reception area looks very nice.
c I managed to get some sleep, actually.
d Mm. You just don't get tea like this in Austria!
e Thanks for coming down to meet me.
f And maybe a glass of water too?
g Where are you now?

Carl   Kathrin, hi. Nice to see you again.

Kathrin Hi, Carl. Nice to see you too.

Kathrin _____ 1

Carl   Always a pleasure! Actually, after the restructuring last year we all got moved around, so I wasn't sure you'd be able to find my office by yourself.

Kathrin Oh, really? _____ 2

Carl   On the fourth floor. They decided to put sales and marketing together – at last!

Kathrin That does make more sense, doesn't it? _____ 3

Carl   Yes, they finally repainted it in June. … Oh, here's the lift now. After you. Was the driver there to meet you at the airport?

Kathrin Yes, she was. _____ 4

Carl   It's the least I could do after your early start! You must be exhausted now.

Kathrin Oh, I'm all right. _____ 5

Carl   Here we are … . So, can I get you something to drink? How about a cup of that tea you like so much?

Kathrin That would be wonderful. _____ 6

Carl   Coming right up. … Here you are.

Kathrin Oh, thank you.

Carl   You're welcome.

Kathrin _____ 7

Look at the dialogue again. What do you say when …

a somebody thanks you? (three answers)
b you want somebody to enter a room or the lift before you?
c you arrive at your office with your visitor?
d you give somebody something?
e somebody gives you something such as food or a drink?

5 Match the questions or comments with the appropriate responses. (Sometimes there is more than one correct answer.)

1 Did you have any trouble finding us?
2 You can leave your bags at reception.
3 We've been in this building since 1985.
4 I'll take you round later to meet the team.
5 Would you like something to drink?
6 Please help yourself to the biscuits.

a Mm, thanks. These look delicious.
b No, thanks. I'm fine.
c That would be nice, thanks.
d Great, thank you.
e No, not at all.
f Really? How interesting.

6 Now work with a partner to make your own dialogue. Decide whether A and B have met before and use appropriate phrases from the box below.

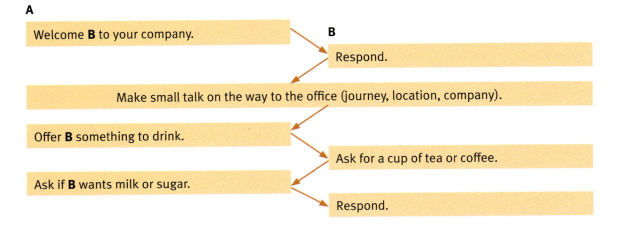

WELCOMING VISITORS TO YOUR COMPANY

Welcoming a visitor
Welcome to [company name].
Did you have any trouble finding us?
Hello, [name]. Nice to see you again.
You can leave your things here/in my office/at the reception desk.
I'll take you around to meet the team.

Offering hospitality
Would you like something to drink?
How would you like that? Milk/Cream (AE)? Sugar?
Here you are.
Please help yourself to the biscuits/cookies (AE).

Talking about the offices and company
It's a lovely space/a very nice location.
The reception area looks very nice.
Have you been in this location long?
How many people work here?
How long has the company been around?

Accepting hospitality
A cup of coffee./Some water would be nice.
Just black./With milk and sugar, please.
Thank you./Thanks.

Try to avoid these common mistakes:
~~Welcome in our company.~~ **Welcome to** our company.
~~Are you in this location long?~~ **Have** you **been** in this location long?
~~We are fifty employees.~~ **There** are fifty employees.
~~Please.~~ *(when you give sb sth)* Here you are.
~~Please.~~ *(when sb thanks you)* You're welcome./Not at all.

UNIT **2** Welcoming visitors | 19

7 Carl is giving Kathrin directions. Listen to the dialogue and complete the sentences below.

1 It's just _____ the corridor, the third door _____ the left.
2 I'll show you _____ it is.
3 But actually, I thought maybe I could just pop _____ Roger's office and say hello.
4 Where is he? – _____ the third floor.
5 So, go _____ the door and turn left to get _____ the lift.
6 Then _____ you come out of the lift, go right, and it's the _____ door on your left.
7 So, I'll meet you _____ here in about ten minutes?

8 You are in your office with a visitor. Look at the sketch below and complete the sentences with the correct words.

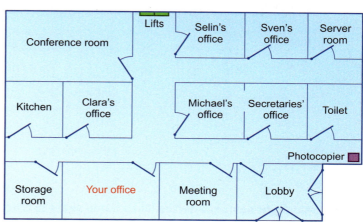

Clara's office ¹?
It's opposite mine.

Go out of the door and turn left. The _____ ² is on your right, just past Clara's office.

Just go out the door and go straight ahead. The _____ ³ are at the end of the corridor.

Go out the door and turn right. The _____ ⁴ is on your left, just after the lobby.

Turn right when you go out of my office. The _____ ⁵ is at the end of the corridor on your right.

9 Work with a partner to practise giving directions. Look at your partner files for plans and the places you want to go.

PARTNER FILES   Partner A   File 2, p. 60
                Partner B   File 2, p. 62

GIVING DIRECTIONS

You just go down the corridor and it's right in front of you/on your left/right.
It's just down the corridor/round the corner on the left/right.
It's the first/second/third door on the left/right.
It's next to the toilet/front door/kitchen.
Come with me and I'll show you where it is!

10 Back in Germany, Lothar Jensburg is introducing Geoff to some of his colleagues. Listen and complete the chart below.

Name	Title
Verena	1
2	product designer
Gregor	3
4	sales manager

VOCABULARY ASSISTANT

gauge *Messgerät*
mix-up *Durcheinander*
specifications *Messangaben*

11 Match the sentence halves. Then listen again to check.

1 The first person I'd like you
2 Verena, this is
3 It's a pleasure
4 Have the two of you
5 It's nice to put
6 Talking of which, this is my
7 I'm sorry, I didn't
8 You'll have a chance

a to meet you, Geoff.
b assistant, Gregor Schieffel.
c Geoff Bacon.
d to get to know everyone better later.
e quite catch that.
f to meet is Verena Fellstein.
g a name to a face, isn't it?
h met before?

ASKING FOR CLARIFICATION

When speaking a foreign language, we sometimes need to ask people to repeat things or to explain what they meant by a certain expression or word.

Asking someone to repeat something:

(I'm) sorry, I didn't quite catch that.
(I'm) sorry, could you tell me your name again?
Sorry, could you say that for me again?

You can ask for clarification with these phrases:

I'm sorry, I don't quite follow you.
I'm not totally sure what you mean.
If I understand you correctly, you would like us to …
Let me see if I've got this right. You would like me to …

UNIT **2** Welcoming visitors | **21**

12 **Complete the mini-dialogues below with words from the box.**

again • are • catch • could • follow • meant • say • see • sorry • sure

A My name is Edward Tsipouri.
B I'm sorry, I didn't quite _____¹ that. Tipori, did you _____²?
A No, Tsipouri. It's a Greek name.

C Excuse me, Mary. Is there a photocopier nearby?
D Yes, it's kitty-corner to Jack's office.
C _____³? I'm not totally _____⁴ what you mean. Kitty-corner?
D Oh, it's … um … diagonally opposite Jack's office. Here, I'll show you.

E I'm afraid John's a bit under the weather today.
F Sorry, I don't quite _____⁵ you.
E Oh, sorry. I _____⁶ that John's ill. He's not coming in today.
F Oh, I _____⁷. That's a pity.

G And I'm Deborah MacGilchrist.
H I'm sorry, _____⁸ you tell me your name _____⁹?
G MacGilchrist. And you _____¹⁰ …?
H Barbara, Barbara Kruger. It's very nice to meet you, Ms MacGilchrist.

13 Think about the people in your company. Make a list of the colleagues you need to introduce to visitors. Now work with a partner. Take it in turns to introduce the people in your company.

INTRODUCTIONS

Making introductions
I'd like to introduce Geoff Bacon. He's the new head of production in London.
The first person I'd like you to meet is [name].
He's/She's our marketing manager.
Verena, this is Geoff Bacon.
This is Marion, our product designer.
This is Heather. She'll be your contact person on the IT side of the project.

Responding to introductions
Verena, this is Geoff Bacon.
– It's a pleasure to meet you, Geoff. *(neutral)*
– Nice/Good to meet you, Geoff. *(informal)*

Have the two of you met before?
– Actually yes, we have.
– No, actually we haven't.

Read the following opinions and answer the questions below.

First names are tricky. Everyone's so concerned about intercultural awareness these days that often you have Americans greeting their Austrian counterparts as 'Mr Dragendorf' and 'Ms Heidenreich', while the Austrians call the Americans 'Bob' or 'Mary' the first time they meet. But on the other hand, hardly anyone is shocked anymore if you don't do what would be normal in 'their' culture.

Visiting companies in the US is always very stressful. People often make little jokes, and I know they're trying to be friendly, but often I don't understand what they mean and then I look like an idiot. I'm sure they think of me as the serious Swiss guy. It's really frustrating.

Coming from Europe, I'm used to being offered a cup of coffee or tea when I visit someone at their company. Perhaps a juice. But I was astonished to arrive at a business colleague's office in Delhi and find a full lunch waiting for me. Have you ever heard of such a thing? I'm not complaining, of course; the food was delicious. Mind you, I don't know what we'll do if the Indian colleague ever visits us!

When you visit someone in a hierarchy-obsessed culture like Germany, it's very easy to tell exactly how important you are to them. Does your counterpart introduce you to her colleagues? OK, not too bad. Does she introduce you to her boss? All right, you can't be that unimportant. And her boss's boss – well, clearly you're someone they're very interested in! But if she doesn't introduce you to anyone, well, that's definitely a bad sign. Germans love making introductions!

Over to you

- What problems have you had using first and last names in other cultures?
- What do you offer visitors to eat and drink at your company?
- Do you find it easier to meet native English speakers or non-native English speakers?
- Who would you introduce to your boss? To your boss's boss?

3 Getting acquainted

Breaking the ice

How well do you know the other people in your group? Ask each other questions and fill in the names of someone who ...

- has a hobby he / she does at least once a week. _____
- enjoys playing a team sport with friends or colleagues. _____
- likes going shopping during the lunch break. _____
- has paintings or photos in his / her office. _____
- never mixes business and pleasure. _____
- has become good friends with a business contact. _____

1 Geoff Bacon is visiting the German company Vierling Design. He and one of the company's product designers, Marion Tischler, are in the conference room waiting for a meeting to begin. Listen to their conversation and correct the sentences below.

1 Anja left the company last June.
2 She lives in Birmingham now.
3 She's working as a programmer for a bicycle manufacturer.
4 Chris is now the marketing manager.
5 He often goes to trade fairs.

2 **Match the sentence halves to form questions from the dialogue. Then match them to the answers (A–E).**

1	Is Anja still	a	doing these days?	A	She's working as a designer for a bicycle manufacturer.
2	That's near	b	you're talking about?	B	It's not too far.
3	Do you know	c	what she's doing there?	C	Exactly.
4	How's he	d	with the company, by the way?	D	She's not, actually.
5	Is that Chris Bennet	e	you, isn't it?	E	He's doing fine.

3 **Here are some more extracts from the dialogue. Complete them with the phrases below. Listen again to check your answers.**

> He says hello, by the way.
> I can imagine.
> Not to worry.
> How's he doing these days?
> That's good to hear.

Marion	Sorry, Geoff, it always takes a few minutes for everyone to arrive.
Geoff	_____ ¹

Marion	I heard from her a couple of weeks ago, and she says things are going well.
Geoff	_____ ² Actually, she did say she wanted to move closer to the sea one day.

Marion	She took us all out on her boat the weekend before she left. It was a lot of fun.
Geoff	_____ ³

Marion	What about Chris? _____ ⁴
Geoff	He's doing fine. _____ ⁵ He was promoted to product manager recently, so he's in the office more these days.

TALKING ABOUT MUTUAL ACQUAINTANCES

Talking about mutual acquaintances *(gemeinsame Bekannte)* is a safe small-talk topic, especially with business contacts you do not know very well:

How's Marita doing these days?
What's Carol up to?
Have you heard anything from Josef recently?
Say hi to Maria for me. (informal) / *Give my regards to Maria.* (neutral/formal)
I'm seeing him tomorrow. Should I say hello from you?

Try to avoid these common mistakes:

~~Greet Helmut from me.~~   **Say hello/hi to** Helmut for me.
~~I haven't seen Claire in the last time.~~   I haven't seen Claire **recently**.
~~What's he making there?~~   What's he **doing** there?

4 Work with a partner to do a role-play. Try to use phrases from the box on page 24.

PARTNER FILES Partner A File 3, p. 60
Partner B File 3, p. 62

> **MOVING FROM SMALL TALK TO BUSINESS**
>
> There is normally a period of small talk at the beginning of a meeting. How long the small talk lasts depends on the culture – it can be as little as 5 minutes or as long as 20 minutes. At some point, the person who is in charge of the meeting should signal that it's time to start talking about business. Normally there will be a short pause in the conversation, then he/she will say something like:
>
> *Well, I suppose we should make a start.*
> *So, shall we get down to business?*
> *Right, let's make a start, shall we?*
>
> Note how words like 'well', 'so' and 'right' are used to show it's time to move on.

5 Talking about what you do in your free time (eg hobbies, sport) is a popular topic for small talk. Complete the free-time activities below by writing in the missing vowels (a, e, i, o, u). Can you add two more activities to each list?

Sport
sk⬜⬜ng
d⬜⬜ng y⬜g⬜
k⬜⬜p⬜ng f⬜t
pl⬜y⬜ng f⬜⬜tb⬜ll
_____
_____

Relaxing at home
l⬜st⬜n⬜ng t⬜ m⬜s⬜c
r⬜⬜d⬜ng
w⬜tch⬜ng t⬜l⬜v⬜s⬜⬜n
c⬜⬜k⬜ng
_____
_____

Going out
⬜⬜t⬜ng ⬜⬜t
g⬜⬜ng t⬜ th⬜ c⬜n⬜m⬜
sh⬜pp⬜ng
g⬜⬜ng t⬜ c⬜nc⬜rts
_____
_____

6 Complete the sentences with the correct form of 'do', 'go' or 'play'.

1 Are there any nice places to _____ running around here?

2 My daughter and I enjoy _____ chess.

3 _____ you ever _____ tai chi? I really enjoy it.

4 How often _____ you _____ to the gym?

5 I _____ the piano since I was a child.

6 Last summer we _____ windsurfing almost every day.

7 I used to _____ aerobics when I was younger.

8 I wish I had time to _____ more sport.

FREE-TIME ACTIVITIES

Asking about free-time activities
So, what do you like doing in your free time?
Do you have any hobbies?
Do you do any sports?
What do you do to keep fit?

Talking about free-time activities
I love/(don't) like/hate cooking/watching TV.
I often go to the gym/do yoga after work/at the weekend.
I like going to the theatre but I hardly ever have the time.
I try to play football/squash at least once a week.

Try to avoid these common mistakes:

I like looking television.	I like **watching** television.
I hate making fitness.	I hate **going to the gym**.
I often go in the cinema.	I often go **to** the cinema.
I like it to read books in English.	I like **reading** books in English.

7 Work with a partner to make a dialogue. A and B are waiting for a meeting to begin and are chatting until the other participants arrive. (A is in charge of the meeting.)

A

Greet **B** and ask how he/she is.

B

Respond. Ask **A** how he/she is.

Respond. Ask about **B**'s journey.

Respond. Say something about the weather.

Respond. Ask about your partner's hobbies.

Respond. Ask about a mutual acquaintance/ a colleague you both know.

Respond. (The other participants have arrived.) Say it's time to begin.

Agree.

UNIT 3 Getting acquainted | 27

8 The meeting participants are having a break. Listen to the dialogues. Who …

- offers Geoff a coffee?
  _____ 1

- needs to go to the toilet?
  _____ 2

- has a friend who is an artist?
  _____ 3

- wants to buy a birthday present?
  _____ 4

- likes opera?
  _____ 5

- went to London on a school exchange?
  _____ 6

9 Complete these sentences from the dialogues. Listen again if necessary.

1 _____ start again at, _____, 3.30?

2 _____ you a coffee, Geoff?

3 That _____, thanks Marion.

4 _____ your toilet?

5 _____ your coffee. _____ black, right?

6 That's an interesting painting you've _____, Lothar.

7 I can give you his phone number _____.

8 Is this your _____ in Germany?

9 Was that for business _____?

10 Have you _____ to England?

ADMIRING PERSONAL POSSESSIONS

In Britain and the USA it is acceptable to compliment your host on personal objects in his/her home or office, and this is a common small-talk topic when visiting someone. However, in some cultures (eg Greece or Thailand), it is better not to admire a personal object openly. If you do, the host may feel obliged to give it to you.

10 Talking about places you have visited is a common small-talk topic. Choose one line from each column to make mini-dialogues.

Person A	Person B	Person A
1 So is this your first time in Switzerland?	a Yes, very much. Especially the food!	A I know. It's terrible, isn't it?
2 Have you ever been to Canada?	b No, this is my first time. What about you?	B That's good. At least you had some time to relax.
3 Did you enjoy your visit to Munich?	c No, it was actually a business trip. But I had a couple of days free.	C Oh really? Was that for business or pleasure?
4 Have you been here before?	d We found this fantastic hotel right next to the river.	D It's my first time here as well.
5 What did you think of Edinburgh?	e Actually, I was here once before, in 2001.	E Sounds great! Do you remember the name?
6 Were you there on holiday?	f It's an amazing city. Pity about the weather though!	F You should. It's really a great country.
7 Where did you stay when you were there?	g No, but I'd love to go there sometime.	G I know, it's delicious, isn't it?

> **KEEPING THE CONVERSATION GOING**
>
> Here are some ways to keep the conversation going.
> - When someone asks you a question, ask them the question back as well:
>   *Have you ever been to Hong Kong?*
>   *No, I haven't.* **What about you?**
>
> - Give some extra information when you answer the question:
>   *I was there in '98.* **I stayed in this great place in the old town.**
>
> - Use question tags to encourage the other person to speak:
>   *The food in France is great,* **isn't it?**
>   *I know. I ate so much when I was there!*

11 Look at the following questions and think of responses that will keep the conversation going.

1 So, have you ever been to Italy?

2 Do you enjoy going to the theatre?

3 Is this weather typical for the time of year?

4 Do you play tennis?

12 **The sentences below are taken from emails Lothar and Geoff wrote to thank each other for the visit. Decide who wrote each sentence, Lothar (L) or Geoff (G).**

- [G] a I hope that I will be able to return the favour
- [ ] b I hope you had a good trip back to the UK
- [ ] c I just wanted to say thank you for inviting me to your company last week
- [ ] d I really enjoyed having you visit the company
- [ ] e I enjoyed the chance to meet your team
- [ ] f Please give my best to Marion, Verena, Matthias and Gregor

Now complete the emails using the sentences above.

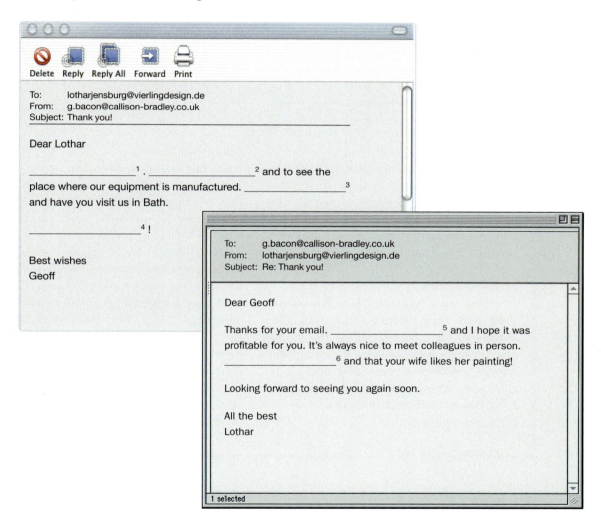

To: lotharjensburg@vierlingdesign.de
From: g.bacon@callison-bradley.co.uk
Subject: Thank you!

Dear Lothar

_____¹. _____² and to see the place where our equipment is manufactured. _____³ and have you visit us in Bath.

_____⁴!

Best wishes
Geoff

To: g.bacon@callison-bradley.co.uk
From: lotharjensburg@vierlingdesign.de
Subject: Re: Thank you!

Dear Geoff

Thanks for your email. _____⁵ and I hope it was profitable for you. It's always nice to meet colleagues in person. _____⁶ and that your wife likes her painting!

Looking forward to seeing you again soon.

All the best
Lothar

13 **Think of a business contact you know. Imagine you have been to visit him/her at his/her company. Write a thank-you email. Use the emails from Exercise 12 as models.**

Wrapping up

Read the following article and discuss the questions below.

Small talk made simple

In theory, making small talk in English isn't rocket science. All you need to do is say hello and ask a few questions: 'Where are you from?' 'Do you like it there?' 'How did you get into engineering/marketing/metallurgy?'

Of course, in practice it can be more difficult. Maybe the person you're trying to speak to keeps replying with one-word answers. Maybe you always seem to meet people in noisy conference halls where you can hardly hear what they're saying, let alone understand it. Or maybe – and this seems to happen to a lot of people – you can talk about your job for hours, but feel much less secure making chit-chat.

What can you do to solve these problems? Well, there are a lot of things you can try.

Watch the pros ...
Observe people who are confident speaking English. How do they talk? Contribute, of course, but listen, and note the questions they ask. Also think about their intonation – the way they use their voice to convey meaning. Is it something you can try yourself?

... and the stars
Of course, your colleagues from London will think you're crazy if you start writing down things they say. "'Please, call me Bill,' did you say? Oh that's quite good ..." But actors don't mind this at all. So the next time you're in the video shop, try borrowing an English-language DVD. Watch it with subtitles, and pay attention to the way people interact.

Listen and learn
While you're at it, do more than watch: repeat what you hear the actors say. Then record yourself and play it back. (Most laptops and MP3 players have built-in microphones.) It might be a bit embarrassing at first, but this is the best way to become aware of your speech and how it sounds to others. Compare your pronunciation to the one on the CD or DVD, and try again. You'll be impressed at how quickly you improve.

Practice makes perfect
Easier said than done, but really: don't be shy. The more you say during the coffee break, the more confident you'll feel about making conversation at lunch.

Over to you

- What tips can you add?
- What ideas have you tried to make socializing in English easier? What has worked for you?
- Do you know anyone who is good at socializing in English? What makes them so effective?

4 Entertaining a visitor

Breaking the ice

Answer these questions about entertaining a visitor and then ask a partner.

	me	my partner
1 Who were the last business visitors you had?		
2 How did you socialize with them? (go for dinner, see a concert, etc)		
3 What did you talk about?		
4 What did you *not* talk about? (family, politics, work, etc)		
5 Was it easy or difficult to look after the visitors? Why?		

15–17

1 Rolf and Jessica are showing their American visitor, Phillip, around their town. Listen to the dialogues and match them to the places on the map.

Conversation 1 ☐

Conversation 2 ☐

Conversation 3 ☐

Read the extract from the tourist brochure. Rolf and Jessica make three mistakes in the information they tell Phillip. What are they? Listen again if necessary.

A **Schwarzburg Arkaden (shopping centre)**
• Built in 2002
• More than 20 shops and restaurants

B **Schloss Schwarzburg (Schwarzburg castle)**
• Built by King Heinrich the First in 1743
• Partially destroyed during World War Two
• Rebuilt in the 1960s

C **Schwarzburg Art Gallery**
• Designed by the American architect Renzo Kindeslieb
• Building was a brewery (closed in 1994)

D **Rathaus (Town Hall)**
• Built in 1834
• Often has exhibitions open to the public

E **Schwarzburg Cathedral**
• Built between 1510 and 1543
• Services on Sundays at 8 am and 10 am

RECENT GERMAN HISTORY

There's no direct translation for *nach der Wende* in English. We say 'after reunification' or 'after the Wall came down' instead.
Here are some other translations of useful words and phrases for talking about recent German history.

DDR	East Germany or GDR
die Mauer	The Berlin Wall
der Fall der Mauer	the fall of the Wall
Tag der deutschen Einheit	Day of German Unity or German Unity Day

15–17

2 Complete the sentences from the dialogues in Exercise 1 using the words below. (There are some words you do not need.) Listen again to the dialogues if necessary.

actually • building • built • designed • destroyed • shut • supposed • telling • that • this • typical

1 _____ is the cathedral here.
2 This kind of architecture is _____ of our region.

3 That's the castle I was _____ you about earlier.
4 It was _____ by King Heinrich the Second.
5 It was almost completely _____ by bombing in the war.

6 Part of the _____ used to be a brewery.
7 The brewery _____ in 1992 after reunification.
8 The building is _____ to look like a beer bottle.

USED TO

We use the phrase 'used to' when we are talking about things which were true in the past but are not true now. We use it a lot when socializing, especially when talking about our lives or the history of our town:
  I used to live in Schweinfurt.
  Part of the building used to be a brewery.
  Brewing used to be a big industry here in Schwarzburg.

'Used to' in English is similar to *früher* in German:
  I used to work at BMW. = Früher habe ich bei BMW gearbeitet.

Note that we don't say 'in former times':
  ~~In former times I worked at BMW~~ → **I used to work** at BMW.

3 Translate these sentences into English.

1 Früher habe ich in München gelebt.   *I used to live in Munich.*
2 Früher hat meine Frau bei Siemens gearbeitet. _____
3 Das war früher eine Fabrik. _____
4 Früher haben mehr Leute in der Stadt gewohnt. _____
5 Früher hatten wir kein Museum in der Stadt. _____
6 War das früher eine Brauerei? _____

4 Talking about the place where you live or work is a popular small-talk topic. Use the following words and phrases to complete the sentences below. You can use some words more than once.

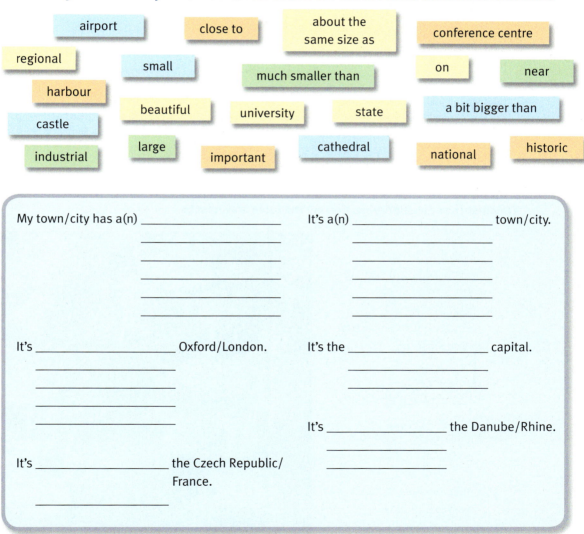

Can you add more words to any of the lists? Now write a short text about your town or city.

> **USING TOURIST INFORMATION**
>
> Many cities have tourist information brochures available in English. Visit your local tourist office or their website to see what they have. Or, if your town or city is popular with tourists, visit travel websites such as www.lonelyplanet.com or www.roughguides.com to see what they say about where you live. It's a good way to learn the vocabulary you need to tell visitors about your town.

5 Imagine you are showing your partner around the place where you live or work. Tell him/her about three sights in your town/city. (If you like, draw a simple map to use as a reference.)

> **SHOWING VISITORS AROUND**
>
> If we go along here, we come to …
> On your left/right you can see …
> The [place] is right in front of you/on your left/right.
> The [name of town/city] is opposite the …
> The castle/church/… was built by … in …
> … is famous for …
> The … is open to visitors from … to …
>
> Try to avoid these common mistakes:
> ~~The town hall is on your right side.~~   The town hall is on your **right**.
> ~~The museum is opposite from the cathedral.~~   The museum is **opposite** the cathedral.
> ~~The theatre was designed from a Danish architect.~~   The theatre was designed **by** a Danish architect.

6 Rolf, Jessica and Phillip are having a coffee in a local café. Listen and decide if the following statements are true or false. Correct the false statements.

1 Both Jessica and Rolf are from Schwarzburg.

2 Jessica went to university in Schwarzburg.

3 Jessica finds Schwarzburg a bit small.

4 Phillip agrees to go to a museum with Rolf.

5 Phillip decides to go to an art exhibition.

UNIT 4 Entertaining a visitor | 35

7 **Match the sentence halves to make sentences from the dialogue. Listen again if necessary.**

1 So are you both
2 How long
3 I went to
4 When I graduated
5 And do you
6 That's something
7 I grew up
8 She was

a like living here?
b university in Greifswald.
c from Schwarzburg originally?
d born in Schwarzburg, actually.
e I moved to Schwarzburg.
f on a farm.
g have you lived here?
h I miss in Chicago.

8 **Work with a partner. Ask your partner some or all of the following questions to find out about their life. Make a note of the answers.**

Are you from [name of town/city] originally?
How long have you lived here?
Where did you live before that?
Did you go to college/university/vocational school in [name of town/city]?
What did you study?
Do you like living here?
Do you ever miss [name of place]?
What do you do in your free time?

I grew up in …

I graduated from [institution] in [year].

I was born in …

I went to university in …

I live in/near/not far from …

Now tell the class about your partner but include three things which are not true. Can the others guess what they are?

For example:
A So Suzanne was born in Vienna.
B That's not true. I think she was born in Salzburg.
A You're right! She was born in Salzburg and moved to Vienna when she was ten.

TALKING ABOUT ORIGINS

Talking about people's origins can be a very complicated and sensitive area. Here are some tips:

- To refer to (for example) a person born in Germany to Turkish parents, you can say 'a German of Turkish descent' or 'Turkish-German'.
- It is very impolite (and offensive) to ask non-white British or American people where they are 'really' from, or to guess where their family is from.
- Americans of African descent generally refer to themselves as 'African-American' (but not ~~Afro-American~~) or 'black'. The words 'coloured' and 'Negro' are no longer used and are considered offensive by most people.
- British people of African or Caribbean descent generally refer to themselves as 'Black British'.
- Remember that the UK is England, Scotland, Wales and Northern Ireland. So a 'British' person can be from any of these countries, and (for example) a 'Scottish' person is also 'British' but not English. Never ask a Scottish person "Which part of England are you from?"!

36 | UNIT **4** Entertaining a visitor

9 **In the dialogue in Exercise 6, Rolf and Jessica also tell Phillip about some things he can do in Schwarzburg. Complete the sentences from the dialogue using the words below. (Listen again if necessary.)**

corner • exhibition • free • lakes • like • museum • next to • nice • recommendations • sounds • take • worth

1 If we have time, perhaps we can show you one of the _____ nearby.
2 That would be _____ .
3 I've actually got the afternoon _____ tomorrow.
4 I was wondering if you had any _____ for things to do.
5 There's a fantastic coal mining _____ just an hour from here.
6 I can _____ you if you like.
7 There's a nice _____ of photos by Ana Witzleben on at the town hall at the moment.
8 It's definitely _____ seeing.
9 That _____ great. I'd really _____ to do that.
10 It's actually just around the _____ from your hotel, _____ the station.

Which sentences are said by …

- the host?   *1,_____*
- the guest? *2,_____*

10 **Work with a partner to practise making recommendations. Try to use phrases from the box on the next page.**

Partner A: Write down three things visitors can do in the town or city where you work or live. Tell your partner what they are and why they are interesting. If your partner wants to see one of the things, then give them directions how to get there.

Partner B: Show interest in what your partner is saying.

Now change roles.

> **RECOMMENDATIONS**
>
> **Recommending places to see**
> There's a(n) great/fantastic/interesting
>   exhibition/art gallery/museum/
>   restaurant/café/shop/park/street.
> It's really worth visiting/seeing/a visit.
>
> **Reacting to recommendations**
> That sounds (really) nice/great/interesting.
> I'll definitely do that.
> I'll definitely go there.
> I'd love to see that.
>
> **Giving directions**
> It's next to/near/close to/just around the corner from the town hall/square.
> It's on the same street as your hotel/the station.
> Just go along this street/Hauptstraße, then turn left/right.
>
> Try to avoid these common mistakes:
> ~~It gives a fantastic exhibition at the castle.~~   **There's** a fantastic exhibition at the castle.
> ~~It's really worth to visit.~~   It's really worth **visiting**.
> ~~It is in the near of the town hall.~~   It's **near** the town hall.

11 Hosts often invite their guests to join them in social activities. Listen to four invitations and complete the chart.

	Conversation 1	Conversation 2	Conversation 3	Conversation 4
a What invitation does the host make?				
b Does the guest accept or turn down the invitation?				
c What excuse does the guest give (if any)?				
d What alternative does the guest suggest (if any)?				

Now put the following words into the correct order to make sentences from the conversations. If necessary, listen again to check your answers.

1 for dinner / if / to join / would like / tonight / us / I was / wondering / you / .

2 meeting / week / How about / a coffee / next / for / ?

3 an / for / have / I / opera / extra / the / ticket / tonight / .

4 come / like / you / to / Would / ?

5 and I / Saturday / are / My / next / partner / a party / having / .

6 come / could / hoping / were / We / you / .

INVITATIONS

Accepting invitations

Here are some phrases for accepting invitations:

That would be lovely.　　　　　*That sounds great, thanks.*
Thank you, I'd like that very much.　　*Good idea. Let's do that.*

Turning down invitations

It is more difficult to say 'no' to invitations and still be polite.
Here are some examples of how to turn down an invitation:

1 thank the person		2 give a reason	3 offer an alternative
That's really kind of you	*but*	*my flight's at 6 pm so I should probably stay in town just to make sure I get to the airport in time.*	*Perhaps we can do it next time I'm in town.*
That's very nice of you	*but actually*	*I'm afraid my boss wants my report first thing tomorrow so I need to stay at the hotel and write that.*	*But maybe we could go for dinner tomorrow instead?*
I'd love to (come)	*however*	*I'm afraid I just don't have time today.*	*How about having lunch sometime next week?*

12 Rewrite B's responses to make them more polite.

1　A　So, shall we have dinner together tonight?
　　B　~~I can't. I have to get up early tomorrow.~~
　　　　That would be really nice, but I'm afraid I have a meeting first thing tomorrow and I have to go to bed early.
2　A　How about some lunch?
　　B　~~No, I don't have time.~~
3　A　I'm having friends over for a barbecue this evening. Would you like to come?
　　B　~~No, I have to prepare a presentation.~~
4　A　We're going for a drink. Would you like to join us?
　　B　~~Impossible. I'm meeting someone else.~~

13 Work with a partner to do a role-play. Try to use phrases from this unit to make and turn down or accept invitations.

PARTNER FILES　　Partner A　File 4, p. 61
　　　　　　　　　　Partner B　File 4, p. 63

Wrapping up

Read this article from an American magazine and discuss the questions which follow.

Making business personal

Business is always personal, and opening up to your business contacts is the best way to develop your business relationships. Kelly Watson argues why you should stop trying to keep your business life and your family life separate.

'Dienst ist Dienst und Schnaps ist Schnaps' is a famous German saying. Work is work, and socializing is socializing, and the two worlds should never meet, right? Wrong! Treating business contacts differently from personal friends is one of the most common mistakes business people make. Think about your business contacts who are also friends of yours. Isn't it easier to do business with them? Don't they help you and tolerate your mistakes more than casual acquaintances? Exactly! So make your business relationships more personal and you will find your work is easier and that you are more successful.

But how can you make business more personal? Easy! Do the same things you would do when making 'real' friends. Show that you're human, not just a face in a suit. Create intimacy between you and the business contact and you will create trust. Instead of just making superficial small talk, talk about the things which are really important to you: your family, your hobbies, your problems and worries.

And don't be afraid to introduce your business contacts to your friends and family. John Zimmerman, who is CEO of a technology company in Seattle and a good friend of mine, began taking his daughter, Laura, on business trips with him so that they could spend more time together. Dinner conversations became more personal because his business contacts wanted to talk to Laura. John's contacts told him about their families, and one manager's son even became Laura's pen friend.

Everyone was a winner with this scenario. Not only did John spend more time with his daughter, but she learned a lot about his work and the world of business. And John's business contacts now invite John and his daughter to spend time with their families, taking those business relationships to another level.

So don't be afraid to mix your business life with your personal life. OK, so you might not be able to give a sales presentation over dinner if your friends or family

are there. But it doesn't matter: when it comes to business, it's the personal relationship that makes all the difference. Mixing your business life with your personal life benefits everybody: you, your business contacts and your family. ∎

Over to you

- Do you ever mix your business and personal lives? How many of your business contacts have met your family or friends?
- Would you ever take a member of your family with you on a business trip?
- Is it easier to do business with friends than casual acquaintances? What are the advantages and disadvantages?
- How can business people balance work commitments with private/family life?

5 Eating out

Breaking the ice

Which of these places would you take the following guests to for dinner? Discuss with a partner.

- a group of British engineers
- an important Indian customer
- colleagues from your American subsidiary
- an international group of young people doing work experience at your company
- a group of high-ranking government officials from Lithuania

Finnegan's Wake

Enjoy the 'craic' at our fun Irish pub!

Large screen TV showing all big sporting events.

Happy hour 7–8 pm every day.
Two pints of Guinness for the price of one.

Zweighof

Traditional German, Swiss and Austrian specialities

—

20 different beers on tap

Large groups catered for

The Bleeding Heart

The best steak in town – cooked at your table.
Special meat buffet on Wednesday nights.
Free side dish with every steak.

FORAGE

Sophisticated modern vegetarian and vegan cuisine in an elegant setting.

All dishes prepared with organic local produce.

Innovative salad and juice bars.

Lee's 'Krazy Karaoke Kavern'

- Fun karaoke bar with over 20,000 songs to choose from!
- Friday night is fancy dress karaoke night - everyone who comes in fancy dress gets a free pitcher of beer!
- Office parties welcome!

Phitsanulok

FINE, AUTHENTIC, FULL-FLAVOURED THAI CUISINE.

We use the very best ingredients with fresh herbs, spices and vegetables sent directly to us from growers in Thailand.

Bulgakow's

Michelin-starred restaurant with award-winning interior.

Seasonal dishes created by star chef André Rogal.

Extensive wine list to complement our meals.

Reservations required

Now think of your own foreign business contacts. Where would you take them? Why?

UNIT **5** Eating out | **41**

1 Jill is in Munich for a meeting with her German colleagues, Franz and Marco. They have taken her to a traditional Bavarian restaurant for dinner. Look at the extract from the menu. Which items do they talk about?

Vorspeisen

Blattsalate
mit gebackenem Schafskäse
€ 4,00

Frische Pfifferlinge
in Rahm
€ 5,50

Klare Tomatensuppe
mit Grießklößchen
€ 3,00

Hauptgerichte

Vegetarische Käsespätzle
mit Salat
€ 8,00

Allgäuer Käseschnitzel
mit Kartoffeln
€ 9,50

Cordon bleu vom Schwein
mit Pommes frites
€ 9,00

Hirschbraten in Rahmsauce
mit Spätzle
€ 12,00

Gebratene Kalbsfiletmedaillons
mit Kräuternudeln
€ 17,00

VOCABULARY ASSISTANT

to be starving (informal)
ausgehungert sein
to be on the tip of one's
tongue *auf der Zunge liegen*
mother-in-law *Schwiegermutter*

2 Match the two halves to make sentences from the dialogue. Listen again if necessary.

1 I'm absolutely
2 I'm afraid they don't have
3 Just say if you need
4 I might need help
5 That's what I'm having
6 You have to
7 You're making
8 I think I'll have that for
9 Do you know
10 Let's see if we can

a catch the waiter's attention.
b English menus here.
c for my starter for sure.
d help with anything.
e my main course then.
f my mouth water!
g with some of this.
h starving.
i try those.
j what you're having?

UNIT 5 Eating out

3 Look at the descriptions of different dishes below. Can you guess what each dish is?

1 So this is a Swiss speciality. You get a pot with melted cheese and then you dip pieces of bread into the cheese and eat them. It's great at parties or when you have a group of people.

2 This is a typical Italian dish. It's made with flat sheets of pasta with tomato sauce in between. It also has a white sauce and maybe some cheese on top.

3 This is an Indian speciality popular in the West, especially in the UK. You have meat or vegetables in a spicy sauce. Often the sauce is made with cream. It's served with rice.

Think of three dishes and explain them to your partner. Can they guess what they are?

EXPLAINING A MENU

This is a(n) Austrian/German/Swiss speciality.
It's typical of/a speciality of our region.
It's a spicy/savoury/sweet dish.
It's a kind of pasta/meat/dumpling.

It's made with meat/fish/vegetables.
It's a bit like spaghetti/pudding/rice/pizza.
It's a light/dark/wheat beer.
It's juice mixed with mineral water.

4 Sort the words below into the correct categories in the table.

bake · sweet · rich · rice · ~~beef~~ · potato wedges · roast · pork · pepper · grill (BE)/broil (AE) · starter (BE)/appetizer (AE) · onion · cabbage · courgette (BE)/zucchini (AE) · salad · main course · chicken · chips (BE)/French fries (AE) · savoury · light · ~~dessert~~ · fry · ham · spicy · lamb

parts of the meal	types of meat	types of vegetable	side dishes *(Beilage)*	ways of cooking	words for describing food
dessert	*beef*				

Can you add more words to the categories in the table?

5 Work with a partner to role-play the start of a business lunch. Explain the menu to your partner and decide what you will order. (Either look at the menu on page 41 or make one up.)

AT A RESTAURANT

Helping with the menu
Let me know if you need any help with the menu.
Oh, that. It's a kind of fish.
It's (a bit) like an omelette.
Do you know ravioli? Well, it's similar to that.
It's made with eggs, milk and sugar.

Deciding what to order
Do you know what you're having?
Have you decided yet?
That's what I'm going to have for my starter.
I think I'll have that for the main course.
I'm going to have the special *(Tagesgericht)*.

Try to avoid these common mistakes:

~~Let's look at the card.~~   Let's look at the **menu**.
~~This dish has flesh in it.~~   This dish has **meat** in it.
~~I don't eat cow/pig meat.~~   I don't eat **beef/pork**.
~~I take the pasta.~~   **I'll have** the pasta.
~~I'd like water with/without gas.~~   I'd like **sparkling/still** water.

6 Jill, Franz and Marco are finishing their meal. Tick the topics they talk about.

the restaurant	☐	friends	☐
holidays	☐	sport	☐
family	☐	cultural differences	☐
mutual acquaintances	☐	their jobs	☐

Now complete the sentences from the dialogue. Listen again if necessary.

1 So, how _____ the Bavarian-style noodles?
2 Oh, they were very _____.
3 So do you _____ here often?
4 What _____ you, Franz?
5 But nowadays, it's a bit _____ to come except for _____ occasions.
6 So are you _____ as well, Marco?
7 You _____ your mother-in-law earlier.
8 Oh, _____. Was the _____ here in town?
9 You'll have to _____ me the photos if you get the _____.
10 So Jill, you were _____ earlier you learned German at school?

7 Talking about your family is a good small-talk subject and helps to develop a relationship. How much 'family vocabulary' do you know? Work with a partner to do this quiz.

A Look at the words below.

> acquaintance • divorced • married • mother-in-law • only child • relations • relatives • separated • single • step-son

Can you find …

1 four words for types of marital status?
_____ _____
_____ _____

2 two other words for 'family members'?
_____ _____

3 words that match these definitions?
a someone who you know but is not a friend
_____
b the mother of your husband or wife
_____
c a girl or boy who has no brothers or sisters
_____
d a son your husband or wife has from a previous marriage _____

B Now complete the sentences.

1 My partner _____ (bekommt) a baby in September.
2 My _____ (Schwager) owns a small shop in town.
3 After the meeting, we plan to meet our _____ (Frauen) for dinner.
4 My _____ (Lebensgefährte) is from Belgium.
5 My son's _____ (Freundin) is studying abroad this year.

8 Work with a partner. Draw part of your family tree with at least five people (or write down the names of five people in your family). Then take it in turns to ask each other questions about your families.

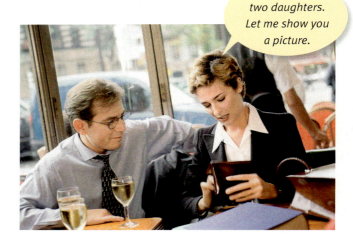

I have two daughters. Let me show you a picture.

TALKING ABOUT FAMILY

Do you have any brothers or sisters?
Is [name] married?
Does [name] have any children?
How old is [name]?
Where does [name] live?

[name] got married in [year].
He/She has … children.
He/She is single.
They are married/living together/separated/divorced.
He/She is … years old.

> **KEEPING A CONVERSATION GOING**
>
> Sometimes it can be difficult to keep a conversation going, especially if your conversation partner is not very good at socializing. Here are some tips for avoiding awkward silences.
>
> - When someone asks you a question, usually it is because they are genuinely interested so don't just give a simple answer. Give some extra information and/or ask another question in return:
>
>   A How long have you been working here?
>   B About three years. Before that I was actually working for the competition. What about you? How long have you been with your company?
>
> - If someone offers 'extra' information when answering your question, ask another follow-up question:
>
>   A This is a great restaurant. Do you come here often?
>   B Oh yes. I was here last week actually.
>   A Oh really? Was that for business or pleasure?
>
> - If the conversation 'dies', you can start a new topic by referring to or asking about something that was said earlier:
>
>   *So, are you married, Marco? You mentioned your mother-in-law earlier.*
>   *You were saying earlier that you spent some time in Africa.*

9 **The answers to the questions below are too short. Make them longer by adding extra information and a question, as in the example.**

1. A So do you live near here?
   B Yes, I do.
   [only 2 km] *Our house is only two kilometres from here.*
   [you / live?] *What about you? Do you live near your work?*

2. A And how old is your daughter?
   B She's six.
   [recently started school]
   [you / children?]

3. A What kind of dog do you have?
   B An Alsatian.
   [fun but needs lots of exercise]
   [you / pets?]

4. A So, how long have you been with the company?
   B Six years.
   [joined after university]
   [you / be with your company long?]

5. A Have you ever been to Moscow?
   B Yes, I have.
   [three years ago / on business]
   [you?]

6. A And do you do any sports?
   B I play squash
   [once a week with friends]
   [you / sports?]

7. A It's so hot today. Is it normally like this in the summer here?
   B No, it's not.
   [very hot for us / usually 25 degrees]
   [weather / where you live?]

10 Commenting on what people say is a good way to keep a conversation going. Match B's comments to what A says. Sometimes more than one answer is possible.

A
1 I just got married last year actually.
2 My husband is a meteorologist.
3 Last year I won a prize for one of the products I designed.
4 The project deadline is next week and we're not going to make it.
5 My daughter has just got a place at one of the best universities in Switzerland.
6 Before I got this job I was unemployed for two years.
7 I went to Peru on holiday last year.

B
a That must be very stressful.
b Really? That's an interesting job!
c Oh congratulations!
d You must be very proud of her.
e That must have been very exciting.
f You must have felt very pleased.
g Oh, I'm sorry to hear that. I imagine that was a difficult time for you.

When do we say 'that must be ...' and when 'that must have been ...'?

11 Work with a partner to make small talk at a restaurant. Use the information in your file to ask questions and keep the conversation going.

PARTNER FILES Partner A File 5, p. 61
Partner B File 5, p. 63

12 Jill, Franz and Marco are ready to pay. Listen and decide if the statements below are true or false.

1 Both Jill and Franz are feeling tired.
2 Franz suggests asking the waiter for the bill.
3 Jill wants to pay for the meal.
4 Jill's company will pay for the meal.
5 Jill wants to pay in cash.

VOCABULARY ASSISTANT
generous *großzügig*
to hit the hay *schlafen gehen, sich aufs Ohr hauen*
to put sth on expenses *als Spesen abrechnen*

13 Complete the sentences from the dialogue with the correct form of the verbs below. (You will need to use some verbs more than once.)

be • catch • get • have • put • round

1. Shall we _____ the bill?
2. Let's see if I can _____ the waiter.
3. Let me _____ this.
4. This _____ on me.
5. That _____ very generous of you.
6. I'm going to _____ it on expenses!
7. You just _____ up the total.
8. I don't _____ any cash on me.

BUT SERIOUSLY …

We say 'seriously' when we want to emphasize that we really mean something (for example when we are trying to persuade someone to accept an offer):

Seriously, this is on me.
Seriously, I can take you to the airport. It's no problem.

We can also say it after a joke:

That's a brilliant suggestion – I'm going to tell everyone I thought of it. But seriously, I do think it's a good idea.
Our lorries are so slow the food is out of date before it arrives. But seriously, we do have problems with delivery times.

Note that in many cultures humour is very important in socializing. But, different cultures tend to have very different senses of humour, and jokes often don't 'translate' well from one culture to another. As an example, the British like self-deprecating humour where a person makes jokes about him or herself. The British can also be very sarcastic in social situations and make fun of each other – to the outsider this can seem rather aggressive.

14 You are in a restaurant in the UK with a business contact and it's time to pay. Work with a partner to make a dialogue.

AT THE END OF A MEAL

Asking for the bill
Can we have the bill, please?
Could you bring us the bill, please (when you have a moment)?

Offering to pay
Let me/I'll get this.
This is on me.

Thanking someone for a meal
That was lovely, thank you.
That's very nice of you to pay.

Responding to thanks
You're (very) welcome.
It was a pleasure.

Try to avoid these common mistakes:

~~I invite you.~~   I'll get this./This is on me./It's my treat.

~~Please.~~   You're welcome. *(when responding to thanks)*

~~The food tasted very well.~~   The food tasted very good./The food was very tasty.

Wrapping up

Look at what these people are saying about socializing in restaurants. Which opinion(s) do you agree with?

I hate it when I'm having dinner in a restaurant with business contacts and it's time to pay. It's never completely clear who's going to get the bill. You have to offer to pay, but then the others have to say that they'll pay. Often I can't tell if they mean it or not, and I don't know if I should pay or let them pay. It's really embarrassing.

Eating with business contacts from another country is very stressful, in my opinion. It's such a cultural thing, and there are a hundred little rules you have to follow, otherwise people think you're impolite. I'm always so worried that I never enjoy my meal!

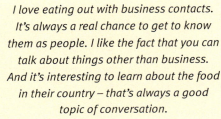

I love eating out with business contacts. It's always a real chance to get to know them as people. I like the fact that you can talk about things other than business. And it's interesting to learn about the food in their country – that's always a good topic of conversation.

Sometimes I find it difficult to know how much to tip when I'm in a foreign country. It's especially difficult when you're not sure how much the money is worth. But normally I ask the people I'm with and they give me some advice.

Over to you

- What other eating and dining habits have you noticed in other countries?
- Who pays when you go to dinner with business contacts?
- How much do you normally tip in restaurants in your country? What about in other countries you've visited?

6 Networking at a trade fair

Breaking the ice

Look at the networking tips below. Do you agree/disagree with them? Which are the best tips?

Steps to successful networking

1 Prepare a 30-second 'verbal business card': "Hi, I'm Shara Lacey. I'm the CTO of GreenFire Systems. We provide …".

2 Offer your name when you introduce yourself. You know who you are, but other people don't!

3 Are you feeling shy and lonely? Look for someone who is alone, and speak to them.

4 Focus on other people rather than yourself. Listen to what they're saying instead of thinking about what you want to say next.

5 Ask questions. You learn more by listening than by talking.

6 Wear comfortable clothes. You won't make a good impression if you don't feel good in what you are wearing.

7 Remember to give people your business card. But ask for their card first.

8 Make eye contact.

9 Smile!

10 Practise! The more networking you do, the better you will be!

1 Here are some topics you can use to begin a conversation at a trade fair. Can you think of any others?

- the weather
- home town / country
- exhibits
- hotel
- practical information (eg asking for directions or help)
- companies
- the trade fair

Now match these statements used to begin a conversation with the topics above. Think of statements for the other topics.

1 I noticed that your name tag says you work for Jansch Networks.
2 Excuse me, do you know how to operate this ticket machine?
3 What a beautiful day! It's too bad we're stuck in here.
4 Are you staying at the Four Seasons as well?
5 This looks very interesting. What is it exactly?
6 Are you here for the electronics show?
7 Excuse me, are you American? I heard you speaking English …

50 | UNIT 6 Networking at a trade fair

2 Ute Adena is the head of purchasing for a large electronics firm in Germany. Listen to three conversations she has at a trade fair in Milan. Which of the topics from Exercise 1 are mentioned? Where is each conversation taking place?

	Topic(s)	Place
1		
2		
3		

VOCABULARY ASSISTANT
to assume *annehmen*
to check out *genauer betrachten*
coincidence *Zufall*   device *Gerät*
POS (point of sale) *Kasse*
tag *Etikett, Schild*

3 Complete these sentences from the dialogues with the words in the box. Then listen again to check your answers.

> about • all • based • checking • do • excuse me • from • join •
> looking after • me • mind • near • noticing • so • sorry • way • with

1 I'm _____, but I couldn't help _____ you've got a Chipper bag.
2 I'm Ute Adena, by the _____.
3 What company are you _____?

4 _____, do you know if this is the stop for the CASPA trade fair?
5 I'm _____ Germany, _____ Frankfurt …
6 So, are you _____ a stand at the fair?
7 Where are you _____?
8 And what _____ you? What _____ you do?

9 Excuse me, do you _____ if I _____ you?
10 Not at _____.
11 _____, when did you get here?
12 That sounds like something worth _____ out.

Which of the sentences 1–12 are used to ...

a start a conversation? _____

b react? _____

c find out more information? _____

> **SAFE SMALL-TALK TOPICS**
>
> Here is a general guide to which small-talk topics are safe and which are unsafe.
>
> **very safe**   **unsafe**
>
> | THE WEATHER | TRAVEL | SPORT | WORK | FAMILY | MONEY | POLITICS | RELIGION |
>
> Of course, safe small-talk topics differ between countries, and also between people. For example, money is a more common small-talk topic in the US than in the UK. And religion is a very 'dangerous' topic in the US, but not so much in the UK. If you're not sure which topics are safe, the best thing is to stay with the very safe topics until the other person introduces other topics.

4 Choose one line from each column to make mini-dialogues.

Person A	Person B	Person A
1 I'm James, by the way.	a Jitterbug Software. We make computer games.	A Well, let's hope the shuttle comes soon!
2 So, what company are you with?	b I think so! I need to go there too.	B We're based in Birmingham.
3 Where are you based?	c No, never. I'd like to go there one day though.	C Thanks. I really need a break!
4 When did you get here?	d Nice to meet you. I'm Susan.	D I arrived late last night.
5 So, are you working on one of the stands?	e Just this morning. What about you? When did you come?	E You should if you get the chance. It's very beautiful.
6 Excuse me, do you know if this is the bus stop for the trade fair?	f In Linz, in Austria. And your company?	F Me too.
7 Do you mind if I join you?	g No, not at all. Take a seat.	G Ah, OK. I think I know the name.
8 Have you ever been to Switzerland?	h No, I'm just here to look around.	H Nice to meet you too.

5 **Work with a partner to do two role-plays that take place at a trade fair. Try to use phrases from the box below.**

PARTNER FILES Partner A File 6, p. 61
Partner B File 6, p. 63

> **STRIKING UP A CONVERSATION**
>
> Excuse me, are you ...?
> I noticed that ...
> I'm [name], by the way.
> Have you seen this before?

6 **Ute is talking to a potential supplier, Thomas Vogt from Xene Electronics, at his stand. Listen and answer the questions below.**

1 What does Thomas want to show Ute?
2 Why does Ute have to go?
3 When does Ute say she will see the product?
4 Do you think Ute will really come back to the stand?

7 **Unjumble the words to make sentences from the dialogue.**

1 probably / kind / I should / that's very / but / get going / of you /.
_____

2 only / it'll / a minute / take /.
_____

3 meeting someone / supposed / actually / in ten minutes / I'm / to be /.
_____

4 a couple / you're / they won't mind / I'm sure / if / late / of minutes /.
_____

5 afterwards / a look / come back / why don't I / to take / ?
_____

6 afraid / really / go / I'm / should / I /.
_____

7 right back / my appointment / come / I'll / after /.
_____

8 then / a little while / you / see / in /.
_____

Who says which sentences above?

Ute: *1,* _____   Thomas: _____

ENDING A CONVERSATION POLITELY

Sometimes it can be difficult to end a conversation politely. Here are some tips for getting away from people without being rude.

- Exchange business cards (this is often a signal you want to end the conversation):

    Anyway, let me give you my card.
    Listen, do you have a card?

- Say you have to leave because of another commitment, eg another meeting:

    Sorry, I really have to go now. My boss is waiting for me outside.
    I should really get going. I have another appointment in a couple of minutes.

- Say you've seen someone you want to talk to:

    Listen, I've just seen Chris over there. Excuse me a moment, I really need to catch him.

Native speakers often use words like 'so', 'right then' and 'OK' (often with the person's name) to signal that they are ready to finish the conversation. The sentence 'It was nice talking to you' is a very clear signal that the person wants to move on.

8 Rewrite B's lines to make them more polite.

1   A   Can I show you our latest product?
    B   ~~No. I have to go. Goodbye.~~

    Sorry. I'd love to see it, but I should really get going.

2   A   Let me get you another coffee.
    B   ~~No, thanks. I'm going to talk to my friend over there.~~

    _____

3   A   Have you seen our new brochure?
    B   ~~No. I have another appointment now.~~

    _____

4   A   Let me introduce you to Sandra, our marketing assistant.
    B   ~~I don't have time. My boss is waiting for me.~~

    _____

5   A   Let me demonstrate our latest software.
    B   ~~Here's my card. I have to go. Call me next week.~~

    _____

9 Work with a partner to do the following role-play.

PARTNER FILES   Partner A   File 7, p. 61
                 Partner B   File 7, p. 63

10 Read this short article from a management publication. Then listen to six extracts from trade fair conversations (a–f) and match them to the strategies (1–6).

Bored with typical small talk questions?

Are you bored with small talk? When you're at a trade fair and have had the same conversation with 20 different people, you don't want to hear the question "Is this your first time in …?" again. And, more importantly, you won't develop those key business relationships if your conversation partner thinks you're boring.

So it's time to get interesting! Here are some strategies that you can use when people aren't interested in the usual small talk questions.

1 Give your (strong) opinion on something connected to the trade fair or situation.
2 Make a joke about something.
3 Talk about something funny that has happened to you during the trade fair (or at another trade fair).
4 Open up to someone by telling them something personal.
5 Show your partner an object you've picked up at the trade fair.
6 Make an interesting observation.

Strategy	Extract	Strategy	Extract
1		4	
2	a	5	
3		6	

Choose three of the strategies above and think of something you can say for each one.
Then make a dialogue with your partner (imagine you are both at a trade fair or another event) and use the three strategies you have chosen.

11 **Complete these sentences from the dialogues with words from the box. Then listen again to check your answers.**

amazes • ever • experience • hand out • hate • imagine • keep • look • weird

1 I've only managed to _____ three business cards.
2 _____ at this amazing pen …
3 It always _____ me at trade fairs how …
4 Isn't that _____?
5 I had this really strange _____ earlier today.
6 Can you _____?
7 This is really the worst-organized trade fair I've _____ seen.
8 I'm sorry I _____ looking at my phone.
9 I _____ being away from home when my kids are ill.

12 **Work with a partner to make small talk during a coffee break.**

A
- Ask **B** if he/she is enjoying the trade fair.
- Comment on the free gift. Give a strong opinion about something connected to the trade fair.
- React. Give some personal information about yourself.

B
- Respond. 'Show' **A** a free gift you got at a stand.
- React to **A**'s opinion. Give some personal information about yourself.
- End the conversation politely.

SMALL TALK AT A TRADE FAIR

Showing someone an object
Look at this … I got it at the … stand.
Look what they gave me at the … stand.
That's really cool/interesting/amazing.

Giving an opinion
I always think that …
It always surprises me that …
The thing about trade fairs is …

Giving personal information
I need to call my husband/wife/son/daughter later.
My … is ill/on holiday/at work.
I talked to my … yesterday and he/she said …

13 Ute has written a follow-up email to a potential supplier that she met at the trade fair. Complete her email using the phrases below.

a do you mind if I ask
b enjoyed hearing about
c hope to see you
d in advance
e put me in touch
f talking to them
g told our head of department
h very nice to meet you
i you could send him
j you mentioned

From: 'Ute Adena' ute.adena@pixdorf.de
To: 'Yves Montrand' yves.montrand@pleinair.fr
Subject: Nice to meet you

Dear Yves

I just wanted to say it was _____¹ at the trade fair last week. I _____² your products and the markets you operate in. I _____³ about your inventory software and he is interested in learning more about it. Do you think _____⁴ some information? His name is Dieter Steinmetz and his email is dieter.steinmetz@pixdorf.de.

By the way, _____⁵ that your company works closely together with GroupSoft. I'm interested in _____⁶ about a possible project – _____⁷ who your contact person there is? I'd be very grateful if you could _____⁸ with someone there. Thanks _____⁹!

Take care, and _____¹⁰ again soon!

Best wishes
Ute

Now write Ute's follow-up email to Per Jensen (see Exercise 2, track 28).

FOLLOWING-UP EMAILS

It's a good idea to write a follow-up email to people you have met at a trade fair when you're back in the office. That way you can keep in touch and make sure they remember who you are. It's best if you have a concrete question or proposal in your email; that way they are sure to answer you, helping to build the relationship. Here are some useful phrases:

I just wanted to ask/mention/send ...
Here is the information we talked about ...
I'd be interested in learning more/hearing about ...
Could you put me in touch with ...?

Wrapping up

Read the article and answer the questions that follow.

How to tell a story or an anecdote in English

One of the hardest skills in a foreign language (or in our first language, for that matter) is telling an interesting story or anecdote. Learners of English often feel left out when socializing with groups of native speakers and everyone else is telling stories except them. It's a good skill to learn – everyone likes to listen to stories and a good storyteller quickly becomes the centre of any group. And talking about your experiences is one of the best ways to build up a relationship with someone.

Fortunately there are some easy ways to make your anecdotes livelier and more enjoyable to listen to. Here are some tips which will make it easier for you to tell stories and anecdotes in English.

Make that link
Try to connect your story to what people are already talking about. There's nothing more boring than a story which is not connected somehow to the present conversation. And it also gives the impression that the storyteller hasn't been listening. On the other hand, a story which illustrates a point you are talking about can be a very powerful rhetorical technique. Use a phrase like "That reminds me of something that happened to me" or "It's funny you should say that because something similar happened to me" to make the connection to your story and begin telling it.

Stay in the present
Use the present tense ("So I say to him …") instead of the past ("So I said to him …"). Not only is the grammar easier, it makes your story more direct and alive. It is very common for native speakers of English to tell stories in the present tense.

Why not use rhetorical questions?
Use rhetorical questions like "So do you know what I do next?" or "And what does she say?" to create suspense and variety.

Get emotional
Talk about what you thought and how you felt at different points in the story ("So there I am in the airport, all alone and feeling like a complete idiot, wishing I'd stayed at home"). It gives the story 'colour' and helps the listener identify with what you are describing.

Use your voice
Vary your voice as much as possible to keep the listener interested: speak slowly or fast, quietly or loudly, in different accents (if you can!). And use timing well – there's nothing more dramatic than a long pause at the most exciting part of the story ("And do you know what was in the box …?").

Over to you

- First listen to this example anecdote. Which tips from the article does the speaker use?
- Now think of something interesting that happened to you or someone you know. Write out the story exactly as you would tell it. Show it to your partner or teacher. Do they have any ideas for making it better? Then tell your anecdote to the other students. Try to tell the story without looking at your text.

Test yourself!

See how much you've learned about socializing and small talk in English. Use the clues to complete the crossword puzzle.

Across

1. Another word for 'talked about': *You ... your mother-in-law earlier.*
4. 'abholen' (two words): *I'll ... you ... at about 7.*
7. One way to take your coffee: *Just ..., thanks.*
9. 'leider' (two words): *... I just don't have time today.*
11. 'kennen lernen': *It's great to finally ... you.*
15. Another word for 'relatives': *I have ... in Stuttgart.*
17. Another word for 'hear': *I didn't quite ... that.*
18. What's the preposition? *I look forward ... seeing you on Tuesday.*
19. What's the preposition? *It's the second door ... the left.*
20. 'eigentlich': *I ... learned German at school.*
22. 'vermissen': *I live in New York City so I ... the countryside sometimes.*
24. Another word for 'very hungry': *I'm absolutely ... .*
25. 'holen': *Can I ... you a coffee?*
26. 'arbeitslos': *Before I got this job I was ... for two years.*
29. Another word for 'very cold': *It was ... in Scotland when I left.*

Down

2. 'Abteilung': *I work in the purchasing ... .*
3. 'dauern': *The meeting should only ... an hour.*
5. Another word for 'nice': *That's very ... of you.*
6. Another way to say 'meet us' or 'come with us' (two words): *I was wondering if you might like to ... for dinner tonight.*
7. 'übrigens' (three words): *I'm Ute Adena, ...*
8. 'Hauptgang' (two words): *I think I'll have the pasta for my ... .*
10. Another American English word for 'bathroom': *Is there a ... around here?*
12. Another way to say 'leave' (two words): *I should probably ... .*
13. A way to say 'früher' in English (two words): *I ... live in Schweinfurt.*
14. 'Ort': *Have you been in this ... long?*
16. 'ursprünglich': *Are you from London ...?*
21. 'Rechnung': *Shall we get the ...?*
23. Another word for 'employees': *How many members of ... do you have here?*
27. 'Ausstellung': *There's a nice ... on at the art gallery at the moment.*
28. What's the preposition? *Shall we get ... to business?*

Test yourself! **59**

Partner A — Partner files

UNIT 1, EXERCISE 5 — FILE 1

Role-play 1
Kris/Kristen: You are meeting Robert/Roberta Brown, a supplier from Britain, at the airport in Frankfurt. You have never met before but have spoken a lot over the phone. Robert/Roberta is carrying several heavy bags. Greet him/her and ask about the flight. Make some small talk (weather, plans for today) and take him/her to your car/a taxi.

Role-play 2
Michael/Michaela: You are visiting the Dutch subsidiary of your company. A colleague there – Daniel/Daniella – is meeting you at the station in Amsterdam. You've met before. Your train was delayed by twenty minutes. There were no services on the train and you would like to buy a bottle of water before you go to the company.

UNIT 2, EXERCISE 9 — FILE 2

You are visiting a company and are in the meeting room. You want to know how to get to different places in the building. Ask your partner for directions to the kitchen, Sue's office and the reception area, and mark them on your plan. Then change roles. When you have finished, check your partner's plan to make sure you gave him/her the right directions.

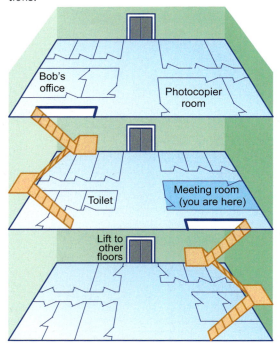

UNIT 3, EXERCISE 4 — FILE 3

You are visiting one of your customers at his/her company. You have been working together for several years and you know a lot of the same people. Ask your partner about his/her two colleagues below. How are they and what are they doing?
- Hilda Pearson
- John Young

Your partner will ask you about these people, who work at your company. (Complete the gaps below before starting the role-play.)

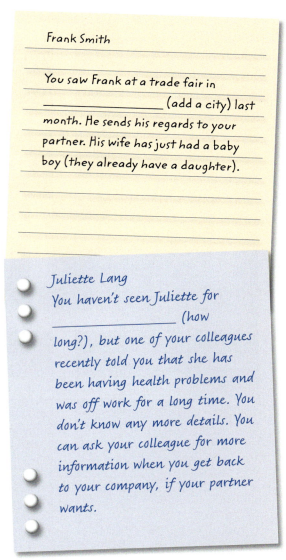

Frank Smith

You saw Frank at a trade fair in _____ (add a city) last month. He sends his regards to your partner. His wife has just had a baby boy (they already have a daughter).

Juliette Lang
You haven't seen Juliette for _____ (how long?), but one of your colleagues recently told you that she has been having health problems and was off work for a long time. You don't know any more details. You can ask your colleague for more information when you get back to your company, if your partner wants.

UNIT 4, EXERCISE 13 — FILE 4

You are looking after a visitor to your town/city. You would like to spend as much time with your business contact as possible. Here are some places you could visit with him/her. Make suggestions about what to do.

City Leisure Centre
Has a huge swimming pool with slides and wave machine. Also squash and badminton courts.

'Hochfeld'
Traditional Swiss restaurant – specializes in cheese dishes – 30 minutes' drive from the city.

Renaissance Theatre
Has a version of 'Faust' at the moment which is supposed to be very good. The play is four hours long.

Jugendstil Café
Historic café built in 1920. One of the big tourist sights in your city. Specializes in cocktails.

UNIT 5, EXERCISE 11 — FILE 5

You are having dinner in a restaurant with an important business partner. (You are the guest.) Ask your partner questions to keep the conversation going.

Here are some things your partner mentioned earlier:
- He/She plays badminton in her free time.
- He/She has an adopted son.
- His/Her mother is visiting at the moment.

Begin by asking your partner a question about the restaurant.

UNIT 6, EXERCISE 5 — FILE 6

Role-play 1
You are standing in the queue to get a coffee at the trade fair café. There are lots of people in front of you and the queue is moving very slowly. However, you have an hour before your next appointment and you are not in a hurry. Start a conversation with the person next to you. You see from their badge that they work for a company which is a potential client for you. Find out who they are and what their position in the company is.

Role-play 2
You work for a company called Tiramax. You are visiting the stand of your competitor Misuto to see which new products they have. They have a very interesting new scanner. Speak to the person on the stand and do the following things.
- Try to find out as much information about the new product as you can.
- Also, try to find out what the company's future plans are.
- Invite the person to go for a coffee so you can talk to them for longer.

UNIT 6, EXERCISE 9 — FILE 7

You are at your company's stand at a trade fair. You are talking to one of your most important clients. It's important to build the relationship and you have to keep the conversation going. Don't let them get away!

Partner B — Partner files

UNIT 1, EXERCISE 5 — FILE 1

Role-play 1
Robert/Roberta: You have just arrived at the airport in Frankfurt and have made arrangements for your business partner, Kris/Kristen, to pick you up. You have spoken a lot over the phone but have never met before. You are carrying several heavy bags. Your flight was fine and you had a DVD to watch. You would like to use the toilet before leaving the airport.

Role-play 2
Daniel/Daniella: You are picking Michael/Michaela up at the station in Amsterdam. He/She works for the German division of your company and you have met him/her before. The train was delayed by twenty minutes.

UNIT 2, EXERCISE 9 — FILE 2

You are visiting a company and are in the meeting room. You want to know how to get to different places in the building. Ask your partner for directions to Bob's office, the toilet and the photocopier room, and mark them on your plan. Then change roles. When you have finished, check your partner's plan to make sure you gave him/her the right directions.

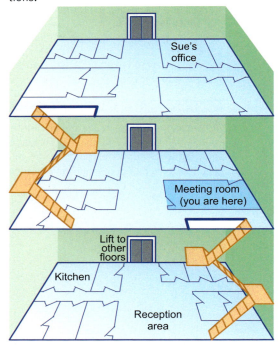

UNIT 3, EXERCISE 4 — FILE 3

One of your suppliers is visiting you at your company. You have been working together for several years and you know a lot of the same people. Ask your partner about his/her two colleagues below. How are they and what are they doing?
- Frank Smith
- Juliette Lang

Your partner will ask you about these people, who work at your company. (Complete the gaps below before starting the role-play.)

Hilda Pearson

Hilda left your company two months ago. You think she has gone to work for a company in _____ (add a city), but you are not sure. You have her new email address in your office, if your partner would like to contact her.

John Young

You have been working a lot with John on a project recently. He is very busy at the moment and quite stressed. He's going on holiday to _____ (add a country) next week and you think he needs a rest.

UNIT 4, EXERCISE 13 — FILE 4

You are visiting an important business contact in another town/city. You would like to spend time with him/her, but you have a lot of things to think about today:

- You have an important presentation to prepare for tomorrow. It will take at least two hours to prepare.
- Today is your son's birthday. You have to phone home this evening to wish him a happy birthday.
- You hurt your knee playing squash last week and you can't sit for long or walk far.

Your partner will invite you to do different things. Respond to his/her invitations. Don't forget the things you have to do today. At the same time, remember that this is an important business relationship and that you have to accept at least one invitation!

UNIT 5, EXERCISE 11 — FILE 5

You are having dinner in a restaurant with an important business partner. (You are the host.) Ask your partner questions to keep the conversation going.

Here are some things your partner mentioned earlier:

- He/She has recently bought a new house.
- His/Her partner has a new job.
- He/She wants to go to Italy on holiday this year.

Begin by saying something about the food.

UNIT 6, EXERCISE 5 — FILE 6

Role-play 1

You are standing in the queue to get a coffee at the trade fair café. There are lots of people in front of you and the line is moving very slowly. You have just given a presentation about one of your company's products to a group of 100 people and are feeling very tired. You really need to sit down and relax. However your presentation went well and you feel satisfied with it. Lots of people talked to you after the presentation and asked for more information about the product.

Role-play 2

You work for a company called Misuto, which you are representing at a trade fair. The person next to you is looking at one of your new products, a scanner. You worked on the project and are very pleased with the product, which is the most modern scanner of its kind on the market. Start a conversation with the person and do the following things:

- Tell them about the new scanner.
- Find out as much information as you can about the person. Are they a potential customer?

UNIT 6, EXERCISE 9 — FILE 7

You are at the stand of one of your suppliers at a trade fair, talking to your contact person there. You are going to change to another supplier soon and you are not interested in talking to the person (who you think is very boring anyway!). Try to get away from them as soon as you can. Use any excuse you can think of!

Answer key

UNIT 1

page 6

1 a is the most formal, b the least

	more formal	less formal
salutation	Dear ...	Hi ...
fixed phrases	Thank you I would be delighted regarding your forthcoming visit	Thanks
closing	I look forward to Kind regards	Looking forward to All the best

2 1 c   2 a   3 b

page 7

1 Have the speakers met before?
   Conversation 1 no
   Conversation 2 no
   Conversation 3 yes

2 Is the conversation formal or informal?
   Conversation 1 informal
   Conversation 2 formal
   Conversation 3 informal

3 Where are they meeting?
   Conversation 1 at the airport
   Conversation 2 at the airport
   Conversation 3 at Clemens' company

4 What problems did the visitors have during the journey?
   Conversation 1 flight was long
       speaker didn't have enough legroom
   Conversation 2 there was some turbulence over the North Sea
   Conversation 3 the traffic was terrible (only one lane open over the bridge)

5 What are they doing next?
   Conversation 1 Alison wants to go to the toilet to wash her hands
   Conversation 2 Ms Metz will take Mr Syms to his hotel
   Conversation 3 they will go to Clemens' office

3 1 must   6 see, again
    2 finally, person   7 waiting
    3 hope, waiting   8 help, bags
    4 pleasure   9 mind
    5 flight

   a 1, 2, 4, 6
   b 5
   c 8, 9
   d 3, 7

page 8

4 1 f   5 a, c, d, h
    2 e   6 g
    3 a, c, h, k 7 g, j
    4 a, c, d, h, k 8 b, i

page 9

6 The topic is the weather.
    1 sunny   6 warm
    2 weather   7 hot
    3 raining   8 cold
    4 terrible   9 down
    5 lucky   10 wet

page 10

7

words describing temperature	words describing the sky	words to do with water
cold	*cloudy*	*damp*
freezing	grey	drizzling
mild	hazy	humid
roasting	overcast	pouring
warm	sunny	rainy

8 (suggested answers)
11:40 Mr Syms arrives at Tegel airport, flight BA120
12 (approx) lunch – *Il Casolare*
2 pm   meeting with sales team
4 pm   visit to production plant
5 pm   Mr Syms back to hotel by taxi
7 pm   pick Mr Syms up for dinner

page 11

9 1 not far, there   6 're going to visit
    2 check into, drop off   7 should only take
    3 can grab, near   8 can take, relax
    4 can go   9 'll pick you up
    5 have the meeting   10 should be, 're going

page 12

11 Across   Down
    3 get   1 freezing
    5 pleasure   2 come
    6 pick   4 great
    7 should   5 pouring
    9 waiting   8 bags
    10 just   10 journey
    11 restroom
    12 delighted

The mystery phrase is small talk.

Answer key

UNIT 2

page 14

1 The topics discussed include the journey, the offices and the company.

page 15

1. Geoff Bacon.
2. No, they haven't.
3. So that he can leave his briefcase and coat there.
4. Six months.
5. It is bright and airy.
6. Ten years ago.
7. 31.
8. (A cup of) coffee.

2
1. Did you have any trouble finding us?
2. The directions on your website were very clear.
3. You can leave your briefcase and coat in my office.
4. I'll take you around to meet a few members of the team.
5. Would you like something to drink?
6. A cup of coffee would be great.

page 16

3

talking about the building	talking about the company and it's history
(ground/first/second) floor	department
lift	employees
location	to expand
to move into	to be founded
neighbourhood	hierarchy
reception	to restructure
stairs	staff

1. location/neighbourhood
2. moved into
3. neighbourhood/location
4. founded
5. employees
6. expanded
7. floor
8. lift

page 17

4
1. e
2. g
3. b
4. a
5. c
6. f
7. d

a Always a pleasure./It's the least I could do./You're welcome.
b After you.
c Here we are.
d Here you are.
e Thank you.

page 18

5
1. e
2. d
3. f
4. c, d
5. b, c
6. a, b

page 19

7
1. down, on
2. where
3. by
4. On
5. out of, to
6. when, first
7. back

8
2. kitchen
3. lifts
4. toilet
5. photocopier

page 20

10
1. marketing manager
2. Marion (Tischler)
3. assistant (to product designer)
4. Matthias (Schulz)

11
1. f
2. c
3. a
4. h
5. g
6. b
7. e
8. d

page 21

12
1. catch
2. say
3. Sorry
4. sure
5. follow
6. meant
7. see
8. could
9. again
10. are

UNIT 3

page 23

1
1. Anja left the company last July.
2. She lives in Bristol now.
3. She's working as a designer for a bicycle manufacturer.
4. Chris is now the product manager.
5. He doesn't often go to trade fairs anymore. / He's in the office more.

page 24

2
1. d   D
2. e   B
3. c   A
4. a   E
5. b   C

3
1. Not to worry.
2. That's good to hear.
3. I can imagine.
4. How's he doing these days?
5. He says hello, by the way.

page 25

5
Sport
skiing
doing yoga
keeping fit
playing football

Relaxing at home
listening to music
reading
watching television
cooking

Going out
eating out
going to the cinema
shopping
going to concerts

6
1. go
2. playing
3. Have, done
4. do, go
5. have played/have been playing
6. went
7. do
8. do

Answer key

page 27

8
1. Marion
2. Geoff
3. Lothar
4. Geoff
5. Geoff (and his wife)
6. Verena

9
1. Shall we, say
2. Can I get
3. would be great
4. Can I use
5. Here's, Just
6. got there
7. if you like
8. first time
9. or pleasure
10. ever been

page 28

10
- 2 – g – F
- 3 – a – G
- 4 – b – D
- 5 – f – A
- 6 – c – B
- 7 – d – E

page 29

12
- b L
- c G
- d L
- e G
- f G

1. c
2. e
3. a
4. f
5. d
6. b

UNIT 4

page 31

1
- Conversation 1 — E (cathedral)
- Conversation 2 — B (castle)
- Conversation 3 — C (art gallery)

1. The cathedral was built in the 16th century (not the 15th).
2. The castle was built by King Heinrich the First (not by King Heinrich the Second).
3. The brewery closed in 1994 (not in 1992).

page 32

2
1. This
2. typical
3. telling
4. built
5. destroyed
6. building
7. shut
8. supposed

page 33

3 (suggested answers)
2. My wife used to work at Siemens.
3. This used to be a factory.
4. More people used to live in the city.
5. We didn't use to have a museum in the town./There didn't use to be a museum in the town.
6. Did this use to be a brewery?

4 My town/city has a(n) airport/castle/cathedral/conference centre/harbour/university.
It's a(n) beautiful/historic/important/industrial/large/small town/city.
It's a bit bigger than/about the same size as/much smaller than/close to/near Oxford/London.
It's the national/regional/state capital.
It's close to/near the Czech Republic/France.
It's close to/near/on the Danube/Rhine.

page 34

6
1. False. Jessica is from a little village just outside Dresden.
2. False. She went to university in Greifswald.
3. True.
4. False. Phillip doesn't want to leave town in case he misses his flight.
5. True.

page 35

7
1. c
2. g
3. b
4. e
5. a
6. h
7. f
8. d

page 36

9
1. lakes
2. nice
3. free
4. recommendations
5. museum
6. take
7. exhibition
8. worth
9. sounds, like
10. corner, next to

The host says: 1, 5, 6, 7, 8, 10
The guest says: 2, 3, 4, 9

page 37

11

	1	2	3	4
a	to go for dinner tonight	to meet for coffee next week	to go to the opera tonight	to come to host's party on Saturday
b	accepts	turns down	turns down	accepts
c		away at a trade fair next week	meeting a friend for dinner	
d		meeting the week after that	going next time host is going	

1. I was wondering if you would like to join us for dinner tonight?
2. How about meeting for a coffee next week?
3. I have an extra ticket for the opera tonight.
4. Would you like to come?
5. My partner and I are having a party next Saturday.
6. We were hoping you could come.

page 38

12 (model answers)
2. That sounds nice, but I'm afraid I'm quite busy today. How about tomorrow?
3. I'd love to, but I'm afraid I have to prepare a presentation for tomorrow. Maybe you'd like to come over for dinner next week?
4. That's very nice of you, but I've actually arranged to meet someone else tonight. Maybe we can go for a drink some time next week.

Answer key | **67**

UNIT 5

page 41

1 They talk about the following items:
   Pfifferlinge, Rahm, (Cordon bleu vom) Schwein, Hirschbraten, Käsespätzle.

2 2 b   7 f
   3 d   8 e
   4 g   9 j
   5 c   10 a
   6 i

page 42

3 1 fondue   2 lasagne   3 curry

4

parts of the meal	types of meat	types of vegetable
dessert main course starter/ appetizer	*beef* chicken ham lamb pork	pepper cabbage courgette/ zucchini onion
side dishes (Beilage)	**ways of cooking**	**words for describing food**
chips/French fries potato wedges rice salad	bake fry grill/broil roast	light rich savoury spicy sweet

page 43

6 They talk about the following topics:
   the restaurant
   family
   cultural differences (different school systems)

   1 did you like   7 mentioned
   2 tasty   8 congratulations, ceremony
   3 come
   4 about   9 show, chance
   5 far, special   10 saying
   6 married

page 44

7 A 1 divorced   2 relations
         married   relatives
         separated
         single

      3 a acquaintance
         b mother-in-law
         c only child
         d step-son

   B 1 is having/is going to have
      2 brother-in-law
      3 wives
      4 partner
      5 girlfriend

page 45

9 (model answers)
   2 She's six. Actually she recently started school. What about you? Do you have any children?
   3 An Alsatian. He's great fun but he needs lots of exercise! Do you have any pets?
   4 Six years. I joined straight after university. And what about you? Have you been with your company long?
   5 Yes, I have. I was there three years ago, on business. Have you ever been there?
   6 I play squash. I meet my friends once a week for a game. And you? Do you play any sports?
   7 No, it's not. It's very hot for us. It's usually about 25 degrees in the summer. What's the weather like where you live?

page 46

10 2 b   5 d
    3 c, e, f   6 g
    4 a   7 e

We say 'that must be …' when commenting on present situations, and 'that must have been …' when commenting on past situations.

12 1 True.
    2 False. Marco suggests asking for the bill.
    3 True.
    4 True.
    5 False. She wants to pay with her credit card.

page 47

13 1 get   5 's
    2 catch   6 put
    3 get   7 round
    4 is   8 have

UNIT 6

page 49

1 1 companies
   2 practical information (transport)
   3 the weather
   4 hotel
   5 exhibits
   6 the trade fair
   7 home town/country

page 50

2

	Topic(s)	Place
1	companies, hotel	at the hotel
2	practical information, weather, home country, the trade fair, companies	at a bus stop
3	practical information, the trade fair, exhibits	in a café at the trade fair

3
1. sorry, noticing
2. way
3. with
4. Excuse me
5. from, near
6. looking after
7. based
8. about, do
9. mind, join
10. all
11. So
12. checking

page 51

a 1, 2, 4, 5, 9
b 10, 12
c 3, 6, 7, 8, 11

4
2 – a – G
3 – f – B
4 – e – D
5 – h – F
6 – b – A
7 – g – C
8 – c – E

page 52

6
1. Their new wireless printer.
2. She has another appointment in ten minutes.
3. Right after her appointment.
4. Probably not!

7
1. That's very kind of you but I should probably get going.
2. It'll only take a minute.
3. I'm actually supposed to be meeting someone in ten minutes.
4. I'm sure they won't mind if you're a couple of minutes late.
5. Why don't I come back afterwards to take a look?
6. I really should go.
7. I'll come right back after my appointment.
8. See you in a little while then.

Ute: 1, 3, 5, 6, 7, 8
Thomas: 2, 4

page 53

8 (suggested answers)
2. That would be nice, but I've just seen someone I really need to talk to over there.
3. Actually, I should get going. I have another appointment in a few minutes.
4. I'm really sorry, but I don't really have time at the moment. My boss is waiting for me, I'm afraid.
5. I'm sorry. I really have to go now. Let me give you my card. Perhaps you could call me next week.

page 54

10
1. e
2. a
3. d
4. f
5. b
6. c

page 55

11
1. hand out
2. Look
3. amazes
4. weird
5. experience
6. imagine
7. ever
8. keep
9. hate

page 56

13
1. h
2. b
3. g
4. i
5. j
6. f
7. a
8. e
9. d
10. c

pages 58–59

Test yourself!

Across
1. mentioned
4. pick up
7. black
9. I'm afraid
11. meet
15. relations
17. catch
18. to
19. on
20. actually
22. miss
24. starving
25. get
26. unemployed
29. freezing

Down
2. department
3. take
5. kind
6. join us
7. by the way
8. main course
10. restroom
12. get going
13. used to
14. location
16. originally
21. bill
23. staff
27. exhibition
28. down

Transcripts

UNIT 1, EXERCISE 2

Dialogue 1

Jürgen Alison Taylor?
Alison That's me. You must be Jürgen.
Jürgen Yes, that's right. Hello! It's great to finally meet you in person after all our phone calls and emails.
Alison Yes, I know. I hope you haven't been waiting long.
Jürgen No, I just got here ten minutes ago. So, how was the flight?
Alison Long! Since the budget cuts, we've had to fly economy and, I must say, I miss the legroom.
Jürgen Tell me about it. Have the airlines forgotten that people are a lot taller now than they were 20 years ago?
Alison Yes, indeed. And we're also quite a bit wider than we were 20 years ago!
Jürgen Right.
Alison At least I had an exit row seat. Anyway, I'd just like to wash my hands before we get going. Is there a toilet somewhere?
Jürgen Yes, there's one just this way …

Dialogue 2

Ms Metz Mr Syms? Hello, I'm Karla Metz from BTO Systems. Welcome to Berlin.
Mr Syms Hello, Ms Metz. It's a pleasure to meet you.
Ms Metz A pleasure to meet you, too. How was your flight?
Mr Syms Uneventful, thankfully. There was some turbulence over the North Sea, but otherwise no difficulties.
Ms Metz I'm glad to hear it. So, if you'll just come this way … . The taxi is over here. I'll accompany you to your hotel.
Mr Syms Wonderful. Is the hotel far from here?
Ms Metz No, not at all. About twenty minutes or so.

Dialogue 3

Anna Hi, Clemens, good to see you again.
Clemens Hi, Anna, good to see you too.
Anna Sorry to keep you waiting. The train was on time but the traffic here is terrible. There was only one lane open over the bridge so the traffic was really slow. The taxi driver said it's been like that for weeks.
Clemens I know, the traffic here is a complete nightmare. I should have told you to take the ring road. Sorry, I completely forgot about that. Anyway, can I help you with your bags?
Anna That would be great. Would you mind taking this? It's the data projector for this afternoon's presentation.
Clemens Not at all. So, my office is just over here …

UNIT 1, EXERCISE 6

Mr Syms I can't believe it's so sunny here. It makes a nice change from England!
Ms Metz How was the weather when you left?
Mr Syms It was raining, as usual! This summer has been terrible.
Ms Metz Well, we've been very lucky here. The last couple of weeks have been very warm.
Mr Syms Do you normally get good summers here?
Ms Metz It depends. Usually we get at least a few hot days, but sometimes it rains a lot.
Mr Syms I imagine the winters here must be pretty cold.
Ms Metz Oh yes. Sometimes it goes down to minus 15.
Mr Syms Well, at least it never gets that cold in England. The winter there is usually just grey and wet. It can be quite depressing!
Ms Metz Ugh! Well, I'm glad the weather is nice for your visit here …

UNIT 1, EXERCISE 8

Ms Metz It's not far now. We'll be there in five minutes.
Mr Syms Great.
Ms Metz So, I thought you might like to check into your hotel first and drop off your things. Then we can grab a spot of lunch. There's a nice Italian place near your hotel.
Mr Syms Sounds good!
Ms Metz After that we can go to the office. We have the meeting with the sales team at 2, as you know.
Mr Syms Yes, that should be interesting.
Ms Metz At 4 we're going to visit the production plant.
Mr Syms Right.
Ms Metz That should only take an hour. Then perhaps you can take a taxi back to your hotel and relax for a bit. I'll pick you up again at about 7 for dinner.
Mr Syms Oh yes, it's the big company dinner tonight, isn't it?
Ms Metz Exactly. It should be really good. We're going to this fantastic Eritrean restaurant. The food there is amazing!

UNIT 2, EXERCISE 1

Lothar Hello, Mr Bacon. I'm Lothar Jensburg. Welcome to Vierling Design.
Geoff It's very nice to meet you. Please, call me Geoff.
Lothar And I'm Lothar, of course. That's 'Lotar', not 'Lothar', by the way. It's a name non-Germans often find hard to pronounce!
Geoff Tell me about it. I've had people call me Ge-off before, so I know what you mean.
Lothar So, did you have any trouble finding us?
Geoff No, not at all. The directions on your website were very clear.
Lothar Glad to hear it. So, if you'll just come this way, Geoff … . You can leave your briefcase and coat in my office, and then I'll take you round to meet a few members of the team. They're all looking forward to meeting you.

Geoff	Great, me too. ... This is a lovely space you have here. Have you been in this location long?	
Lothar	No, we actually just moved into this building six months ago.	
Geoff	Well, it's really nice – very bright and airy.	
Lothar	Yes, it's a huge improvement on our previous building, that's for sure.	
Geoff	How long has your company been around, anyway? I should probably know that, shouldn't I?	
Lothar	Well, the company was founded by Detlef Vierling ten years ago. He was a very successful product designer for the American company IDEO, and he wanted to start something similar here in Germany.	
Geoff	Ah, OK. And how many people are in the company now? I only know the team I work with – you know, you, Marion, Gregor and the others. But it looks like there are quite a few people here.	
Lothar	Yes, we've really expanded over the last few years – in contrast to most German companies, I suppose. We currently have 31 employees.	
Geoff	That's a good number. Not too small, but you still know everyone, I suppose.	
Lothar	Exactly. I'm very happy working here. So, Geoff, before we meet the others, would you like something to drink? Tea, coffee, water, juice ...?	
Geoff	A cup of coffee would be great. I had an early start this morning.	
Lothar	No problem. How do you take it? Milk, sugar ...?	
Geoff	Just black, thanks.	

UNIT 2, EXERCISE 4

Carl	Kathrin, hi. Nice to see you again.
Kathrin	Hi, Carl. Nice to see you too. Thanks for coming down to meet me.
Carl	Always a pleasure! Actually, after the restructuring last year we all got moved around, so I wasn't sure you'd be able to find my office by yourself.
Kathrin	Oh, really? Where are you now?
Carl	On the fourth floor. They decided to put sales and marketing together – at last!
Kathrin	That does make more sense, doesn't it? And the reception area looks very nice.
Carl	Yes, they finally repainted it in June. ... Oh, here's the lift now. After you. ... Was the driver there to meet you at the airport?
Kathrin	Yes, she was. Thanks so much for arranging that.
Carl	It's the least I could do after your early start! You must be exhausted now.
Kathrin	Oh, I'm all right. I managed to get some sleep, actually.
Carl	Here we are ... . So, can I get you something to drink? How about a cup of that tea you like so much?
Kathrin	That would be wonderful. And maybe a glass of water too?
Carl	Coming right up. ... Here you are.
Kathrin	Oh, thank you.
Carl	You're welcome.
Kathrin	Mm. You just don't get tea like this in Austria!

UNIT 2, EXERCISE 7

Carl	Oh, Kathrin, would you mind waiting in my office for a few minutes? I just need to speak to a colleague before he leaves for Manchester this afternoon.
Kathrin	No problem, Carl. But where is your office now?
Carl	Oh, of course, you haven't been there yet. It's just down the corridor, the third door on the left. But come with me and I'll show you where it is.
Kathrin	Great. I'll just leave my bag here, if that's OK with you. But actually, I thought maybe I could just pop by Roger's office and say hello.
Carl	Oh, yeah. I'm sure he'd like to see you.
Kathrin	Where is he?
Carl	On the third floor. So, go out of the door and turn left to get to the lift. Then when you come out of the lift, go right, and it's the first door on your left. His name is on the door.
Kathrin	Great. So, I'll meet you back here in about ten minutes?
Carl	Sounds good. See you soon!

UNIT 2, EXERCISE 10

Lothar	All right, well, the first person I'd like you to meet is Verena Fellstein. She's our marketing manager. Verena, this is Geoff Bacon.
Verena	It's a pleasure to meet you, Geoff.
Geoff	Nice to meet you too.
Lothar	And this is Marion Tischler, our product designer. Have the two of you met before?
Geoff	No, we haven't actually, but we've exchanged a lot of emails.
Marion	It's great to finally meet you. It's nice to put a name to a face, isn't it?
Geoff	It certainly is. By the way, I really liked the prototype you sent us for the new gauge.
Marion	Oh, I'm glad to hear that. We're very happy with it too.
Lothar	Yes, Marion's got a great team working with her.
Marion	I know. I'm very lucky. Talking of which, this is my assistant, Gregor Schieffel – I think you've had contact with him, haven't you?
Geoff	Ah, nice to meet you, Gregor. I'm always sending you faxes, aren't I?
Gregor	That's right. Good to meet you, Mr Bacon.
Geoff	Please, call me Geoff. Sorry about the mix-up with the specifications, by the way. We had a bit of a crisis back in Bath ...
Gregor	No problem. I'm just glad everything worked out.
Lothar	And finally, this is Matthias Schulz, our sales manager.
Geoff	I'm sorry, I didn't quite catch that.
Matthias	Matthias. Nice to meet you, Geoff.
Geoff	Nice to meet you too.
Lothar	Well, I won't ask you to remember all of that. But you'll have a chance to get to know everyone better later.
Geoff	Sounds good. I'm afraid I'm not very good with names.
Lothar	I know what you mean. So, shall we get some lunch?
Geoff	Sounds even better.

UNIT 3, EXERCISE 1

Marion Sorry, Geoff, it always takes a few minutes for everyone to arrive.
Geoff Not to worry. Is Anja still with the company, by the way? I didn't see her when Lothar was showing me around.
Marion She's not, actually. She left last July. As a matter of fact she's in Bristol now. That's near you, isn't it?
Geoff It's not too far. Interesting … I should send her an email. Do you know what she's doing there?
Marion She's working as a designer for a bicycle manufacturer. I heard from her a couple of weeks ago, and she says things are going well.
Geoff That's good to hear. Actually, she did say she wanted to move closer to the sea one day. She enjoys sailing, doesn't she?
Marion That's right. She took us all out on her boat the weekend before she left. It was a lot of fun.
Geoff I can imagine.
Marion What about Chris? How's he doing these days?
Geoff He's doing fine. He says hello, by the way. He was promoted to product manager recently, so he's in the office more these days.
Verena Oh, is that Chris Bennett you're talking about?
Geoff Exactly.
Verena Ah, that explains why I never see him at the trade fairs anymore!
Lothar Hi, everyone, sorry I'm a bit late. Just needed to gather some files for our meeting. So, if everyone would like to take a copy of today's agenda …

UNIT 3, EXERCISE 8

1
Lothar So, shall we start again at, say, 3.30?
Geoff Sounds good.
Marion Fine by me. Can I get you a coffee, Geoff?
Geoff Yeah, that would be great, thanks Marion. Can I just nip to the loo first, though?
Marion Sorry?
Geoff Can I use your toilet?
Marion Oh, of course. It's just down the corridor, second door on the left.
Geoff Great, thanks.

2
Marion Here's your coffee. Just black, right?
Geoff That's right, thanks. That's an interesting painting you've got there, Lothar.
Lothar Yes, a friend of mine did it.
Geoff Really? It's very colourful.
Lothar That's his speciality. He's quite well known here in the area.
Geoff Does he do smaller ones as well? It's my wife's birthday next month and I know she would like his style.
Lothar Sure, I can give you his phone number if you like. Just wait a second while I try to find it …

3
Verena So Geoff, is this your first time in Germany?
Geoff Actually, no, I've been here a few times.
Verena Oh really? Was that for business or pleasure?
Geoff Both. At my old company we did a lot of business with a firm in Stuttgart, so I went over there a few times. And I've been to Bayreuth a couple of times.
Verena Bayreuth?
Geoff Yes, to the Wagner festival. My wife and I are huge opera fans.
Verena That's interesting.
Geoff What about you? Have you ever been to England?
Verena Just once, when I was a teenager. I did a school exchange to London.
Geoff Uh huh. And did you like it?
Verena Yes, although I found London a bit big. I'm more of a small-town person myself …

UNIT 4, EXERCISE 1

1
Jessica And then this is the cathedral here. This kind of architecture is typical of our region.
Phillip Wow. It's really impressive. How old is it?
Jessica Oh, I should know that … I think it's from the 15th century but I'm not totally sure. We can go inside and check if you like?
Phillip Oh, it's not so important. I mean, it might be nice to …

2
Rolf That's the castle I was telling you about earlier. It was built by King Heinrich the Second. In German it's called a 'Schloss'.
Phillip Ah, that's what 'Schloss' means. I saw it on a sign back there. It really is beautiful.
Rolf Well, actually it was almost completely destroyed by bombing in the war and then rebuilt in the 1960s. So it's not all as old as it looks.
Phillip It's terrible how many historic buildings were damaged in the war.
Rolf Oh, that was all a long time ago …

3
Jessica Now this is something we're really proud of. It's our town's new art gallery.
Phillip My goodness. I've never seen a building like that before.
Jessica It was designed by the American architect Renzo Kindeslieb. Part of the building used to be a brewery. Brewing used to be a big industry here in Schwarzburg.
Phillip Really? Do they still make beer here?
Jessica Not any more. The brewery shut in 1992 after reunification. Anyway, the building is supposed to look like a beer bottle.
Phillip Oh yes, I see that now.
Jessica It's good, isn't it? He actually won a prize for it.
Phillip I don't understand why it doesn't fall over.
Jessica Neither do I. It's amazing, isn't it?

UNIT 4, EXERCISE 6

Phillip So are you both from Schwarzburg originally?
Rolf I am, but Jessica is from Dresden.
Jessica Well, a little village just outside Dresden, actually. But I normally say I'm from Dresden because it's easier.
Phillip Ah, OK. So how long have you lived here?
Jessica Seven years. I went to university in Greifswald and then when I graduated I moved to

		Schwarzburg because of my boyfriend. He's from here.
Phillip		And do you like living here?
Jessica		I do. I mean, it's maybe a bit on the small side and there's not much nightlife, but the quality of life is really good here. And it's really nice that you can be out in the countryside in just thirty minutes.
Phillip		Yeah, that's something I miss in Chicago. I grew up on a farm so I miss the countryside sometimes.
Jessica		Interesting. Well, if we have time, perhaps we can show you one of the lakes nearby. They're really beautiful.
Phillip		That would be nice. I've actually got the afternoon free tomorrow and I was wondering if you had any recommendations for things to do.
Rolf		There's a fantastic coal mining museum just an hour from here. It's very interesting. I can take you if you like.
Phillip		Well, that's very kind of you, but my flight's at 6 pm so I should probably stay in town just to make sure I get to the airport in time.
Jessica		I know what you can do. There's a nice exhibition of photos by Ana Witzleben on at the town hall at the moment. It's definitely worth seeing.
Phillip		Ana Witzleben? Wow, she's quite famous.
Jessica		Yes, she was born in Schwarzburg, actually.
Phillip		I didn't know that. That sounds great. I'd really like to do that. Where is the town hall exactly?
Jessica		It's actually just around the corner from your hotel, next to the station.

UNIT 4, EXERCISE 11

19 1 A I was wondering if you would like to join us for dinner tonight?
       B That sounds really nice. Thanks very much.

20 2 A How about meeting for a coffee next week?
       B I'd love to but I'm actually away at a trade fair all next week. How about the week after that?

21 3 A I have an extra ticket for the opera tonight. Would you like to come?
       B That's very kind of you but I'm meeting a friend for dinner this evening. Maybe you can let me know next time you're going?

22 4 A My partner and I are having a party next Saturday. We were hoping you could come.
       B Thanks, I'd like that very much.

UNIT 5, EXERCISE 1

23
Jill	Well, I'm excited about the food. I have to say it's been a long time since lunch – I'm absolutely starving.
Marco	Just as well. The portions are pretty enormous here in Bavaria. I'm afraid they don't have English menus here, but just say if you need help with anything.
Jill	Well, I did some German at school so I'm OK with the basics, but I might need help with some of this. Let me see … 'Frische Pfifferlinge in Rahm'? Is that some kind of meat?
Marco	No, that's actually a kind of mushroom. Oh, what are they called in English? Do you know, Franz?
Franz	Someone told me once. It's on the tip of my tongue. Oh, that's really annoying … . The name sounds French.
Marco	It's a wild mushroom, I think it grows in forests.
Jill	Chanterelle mushrooms?
Franz	Yes, that's it.
Jill	Oh, that sounds good. And what's 'Rahm'?
Marco	That's cream.
Jill	Chanterelle mushrooms in cream? Yup! That's what I'm having for my starter for sure. Now, let's see… 'Schwein' is pork, right?
Marco	That's right.
Jill	Oh, what's this? 'Hirschbraten'?
Marco	That's a meat dish. I'm actually vegetarian, so I don't know the words for these things in English. Franz, do you know what that's called?
Franz	Let me think … Well, 'Hirsch' is deer, and 'braten' is roast, so I suppose it's roast deer?
Jill	Ah, OK. We actually say venison for the meat. Deer is the animal.
Franz	Ah, so you have different words for the animal and the meat in English?
Jill	Yes, we don't like to think too much about what we're eating. So that comes with 'Spätzle', what's that?
Marco	Oh, you have to try those. That's a real Bavarian speciality. They are egg noodles.
Jill	Like Asian noodles?
Marco	No, more like a thick home-made pasta. They're really good. The ones my mother-in-law makes are fantastic.
Jill	Hm, you're making my mouth water! I think I'll have that for my main course then.
Franz	Great. Marco, do you know what you're having?
Marco	Yeah, I think so. I'm going to have the cheese Spätzle. Talking about them has made me want to have some!
Franz	OK, well let's see if we can catch the waiter's attention. They're always so busy in here …

UNIT 5, EXERCISE 6

24
Jill	Phew! That was delicious but if I eat any more I'm going to explode.
Franz	So, how did you like the Bavarian-style noodles, Jill?
Jill	You mean the … er … 'Spätzle'? Is that right? Oh, they were very tasty.
Franz	I'm glad to hear it. Well, if nobody wants the rest of the potatoes, I'll just finish them up.
Marco	I don't know how you can eat so much, Franz! I'm absolutely stuffed.
Franz	Years of practice, Marco. Years of practice.
Jill	So do you come here often?
Marco	Usually just when I have guests. The food's a bit heavy for every day.
Jill	What about you, Franz?
Franz	I used to come here a lot when I worked in the centre of town. But nowadays it's a bit far to come except for special occasions. Anyway my wife is trying to make me eat better these days.
Jill	Oh really?
Franz	Yes, it's all salads and fish at home. That's why it's nice to come here for a bit of red meat.

	Jill	So are you married as well, Marco? You mentioned your mother-in-law earlier.		

UNIT 6, EXERCISE 2

1

Jill: So are you married as well, Marco? You mentioned your mother-in-law earlier.
Marco: Yes, I just got married last year actually.
Jill: Oh, congratulations. Was the ceremony here in town?
Marco: No, we got married in a tiny church up in the mountains. It was lovely.
Jill: That sounds great. You'll have to show me the photos if you get the chance.
Marco: Sure. I have some on my computer in the office. I can show you tomorrow if you like.
Jill: That would be nice.
Marco: Great.

Marco: So Jill, you were saying earlier you learned German at school?
Jill: Yeah, I actually have a GCSE in German. Not that you would know it!
Franz: What do you mean? Your German's not bad at all! But what is a GCSE?
Jill: It's an exam we do at school in England, normally at the age of 16.
Franz: Ah, OK.
Jill: What sort of exams do you do here?

UNIT 5, EXERCISE 12

Jill: Well, I don't know about you two, but I'm ready to hit the hay.
Franz: Sorry?
Jill: You know, I'm tired, ready for bed.
Franz: Ah, I know, it's been a long day, hasn't it? I'm pretty tired myself.
Marco: Shall we get the bill?
Jill: Good idea.
Marco: Let's see if I can catch the waiter …

Waiter: Bitte sehr, Ihre Rechnung.
Marco: Vielen Dank.
Jill: Let me get this.
Marco: No, it's OK. I'll get it.
Jill: Seriously though, this is on me. You two have been paying for everything.
Marco: Are you sure?
Jill: Absolutely.
Franz: That's very generous of you.
Jill: Not really. I'm going to put it on expenses!
Franz: Seriously though, thanks for the meal. It was really nice.
Jill: You're very welcome. Now, what do I do about tipping?
Franz: Tipping?
Jill: You know, leaving some money for the waiter?
Franz: Oh, I see. You just round up the total. I normally leave between five and ten per cent. When you hand the money to the waiter you say the total including the tip, then they give you your change.
Jill: Oh. I was actually going to pay with my credit card. I don't have any cash on me.
Marco: Credit card? In here? You'll be lucky. Maybe we should pay after all …

UNIT 6, EXERCISE 2

1

Ute: I'm sorry, but I couldn't help noticing you've got a Chipper bag. Do you work for them?
Lloyd: No, actually, they're one of our suppliers.
Ute: What a coincidence – they're one of our suppliers too. I'm Ute Adena, by the way.
Lloyd: Lloyd Roberts. Nice to meet you. So, Ute, what company are you with?
Ute: I'm the head of purchasing at Pixdorf. We make software for retail POS systems.
Lloyd: Oh yes, I've heard of your company before. Am I right in thinking you're based in Frankfurt?
Ute: Yes. Well, just outside Frankfurt actually, in a little place called Bad Homburg.
Lloyd: Right.
Ute: And who do you work for?
Lloyd: I work in the purchasing department of a small company called Specialized Solutions in Birmingham.
Ute: Right. I don't think I've come across them before.
Lloyd: So I assume you're here for the trade fair?
Ute: Yes, exactly.
Lloyd: This is quite a nice hotel, isn't it?
Ute: Oh, it is. The breakfast this morning was delicious.

2

Ute: Excuse me, do you know if this is the stop for the CASPA trade fair?
Yves: Yes, it is. The next bus should be arriving in five minutes.
Ute: Great. What a beautiful day!
Yves: Yes, it is, isn't it? In France it was raining all last week, so this is a nice change.
Ute: I know. I'm from Germany, near Frankfurt, and it was actually snowing when I left.
Yves: Ugh! … So, are you looking after a stand at the fair?
Ute: No, I'm actually just here to look around and do some networking, you know. What about you?
Yves: We have a stand here. I'm with a French company called Plein Air, and we're introducing new inventory software.
Ute: Oh, that sounds interesting. Where are you based?
Yves: In Toulouse. Do you know it?
Ute: Oh, yes. I visited Toulouse and the area last summer, actually. It's a wonderful part of France. Airbus has its HQ there, right?
Yves: That's right. It's the backbone of the city's industrial base, in fact the whole region's. And what about you? What do you do?
Ute: I'm the head of purchasing at Pixdorf.
Yves: And that's near Frankfurt, you said?
Ute: Exactly – Bad Homburg. Have you ever been to Germany?
Yves: Only once, on a school exchange. I keep meaning to visit, though. Ah, here's our bus!
Ute: Great.
Yves: Please, after you …

3

Ute Excuse me, do you mind if I join you?
Per Not at all.
Ute I'm Ute Adena.
Per Nice to meet you. I'm Per Jensen.
Ute Nice to meet you too. ... Do you know if it's table service here or do we have to go to the counter?
Per It's table service. So you can sit back and relax!
Ute Yeah, I really need a break. So, when did you get here?
Per On Monday. And you?
Ute Just today, actually. So, what do you think of the fair so far?
Per It's quite good. Certainly better than last year.
Ute Have you seen anything interesting?
Per Well, one company has developed a really nice security device for clothing. It's very secure, but doesn't damage clothing the way current tags do. That's always a real headache for us.
Ute Really? That sounds like something worth checking out.
Per Well, if you want to take a look, just go to section B. The stand is right near the door.
Ute Thanks for the tip!

UNIT 6, EXERCISE 6

Thomas So you see we really have some very exciting new products.
Ute They're certainly very interesting. Anyway, let me give you my card.
Thomas Thank you. Now, I absolutely have to show you our new wireless printer. Let me just get it for you ...
Ute Listen, that's very kind of you but I should probably get going.
Thomas It'll only take a minute. It's really one of our most interesting developments.
Ute I'd love to see it but I should really get going. I'm actually supposed to be meeting someone in ten minutes.
Thomas Oh, I'm sure they won't mind if you're a couple of minutes late ...
Ute Why don't I come back afterwards to take a look?
Thomas Well, if you're sure you don't have time.
Ute No, I'm afraid I really should go. I'll come right back after my appointment.
Thomas Great. I'll be here.
Ute See you in a little while then.
Thomas See you later.

UNIT 6, EXERCISE 10

a Oh no, it's the last day of the fair and I've only managed to hand out three business cards. That means I've got to get rid of 197 today or my boss'll kill me! Perhaps I'll just give one to everyone on the plane back to Munich tonight!

b Look at this amazing pen I got at the Sony stand. It's also a voice recorder. I can't believe they give away such cool stuff these days.

c It always amazes me at trade fairs how people carry around these ugly free bags. They're wearing their best thousand-euro suits but they have these one-euro bags they've got from the sponsor. Isn't that weird?

d I had this really strange experience earlier today. I was in the bathroom washing my hands, and this guy comes up to me and tries to give me his business card. In the bathroom! Can you imagine?

e This is really the worst-organized trade fair I've ever seen. My five-year-old son could do a better job of running it.

f I'm sorry I keep looking at my phone. My daughter is ill today and my husband is at home looking after her. I'm waiting for him to call me to tell me how she is. I hate being away from home when my kids are ill.

UNIT 6, WRAPPING UP

... that reminds me of something really embarrassing that happened to me last year. I'm supposed to be going to a food trade fair in Frankfurt. My secretary's got everything organized – flights, hotel, everything. I'm feeling pretty pleased with myself and looking forward to a weekend away with lots of nice German beer.

Anyway, I arrive in Frankfurt and get into a taxi at the airport. First problem: the taxi driver, this young Russian guy, has never heard of my hotel. He spends half an hour on the phone to his headquarters and eventually finds another hotel with a similar name. We decide my secretary must have written the name down wrong, and we set off to this hotel.

So we arrive there, this really run-down place in the middle of nowhere, and I'm thinking, why has my secretary checked me into this dump? I pay the driver 50 euros for the fare – the whole thing has taken an hour already, and I feel like this guy is my friend – and I go into this horrible hotel. They have this terrible 1970s carpet in the reception and my feet are sticking to it. By this time I'm not feeling very happy.

Anyway, I go up to the desk, and what do you think they say? They've never heard of me and don't have a reservation in my name. I feel like I'm in a bad dream. I try to call my secretary but of course she's out having fun – it's Friday night – and I just get her voicemail.

Well, I'm exhausted and I just want to have a large whisky and go to bed, so I decide to stay at this horrible hotel. I book myself in and ask them to reserve me a taxi for the morning. They ask where I want to go and I say I'm going to the food trade fair. The receptionist starts laughing. I ask her what's so funny. And do you know what she says? I'm in the wrong Frankfurt. I'm in Frankfurt am Main, but the trade fair is in Frankfurt an der Oder, on the other side of Germany ...

A–Z word list

A
acquainted, to get ~ [get ə'kweɪntɪd]	sich kennen lernen	Coming right up. [ˌkʌmɪŋ ˌraɪt 'ʌp]	Kommt sofort! Schon erledigt!
to admire [əd'maɪə]	bewundern	commitment [kə'mɪtmənt]	Engagement, Einsatz; Verabredung
advance, in ~ [ɪn əd'vɑːns]	im Voraus	common myth [ˌkɒmən 'mɪθ]	verbreiteter Mythos, gängiges Vorurteil
advice [əd'vaɪs]	Ratschlag		
airy, to be ~ [bi 'eəri]	hier: geräumig sein	competition [ˌkɒmpə'tɪʃn]	Konkurrenz
amazing [ə'meɪzɪŋ]	erstaunlich, unglaublich	to complain [kəm'pleɪn]	sich beschweren, sich beklagen
annoying, to be ~ [bi ə'nɔɪɪŋ]	ärgerlich, unangenehm sein	concerned, to be ~ [bi kən'sɜːnd]	besorgt sein
to apologize [ə'pɒlədʒaɪz]	sich entschuldigen	confident, to be ~ [bi 'kɒnfɪdənt]	selbstsicher, selbstbewusst sein
appetizer (AE) ['æpɪtaɪzə]	Vorspeise		
arrangements, to make ~ [meɪk ə'reɪndʒmənts]	Vorbereitungen treffen	contact person ['kɒntækt ˌpɜːsn]	Ansprechpartner/in
art gallery ['ɑːt ˌgæləri]	Kunstgalerie	contrast to, in ~ [ɪn 'kɒntrɑːst tə]	im Gegensatz zu
astonished, to be ~ [bi ə'stɒnɪʃt]	erstaunt sein	to contribute [kən'trɪbjuːt]	etw beitragen
attention, to catch sb's ~ [ˌkætʃ ə'tenʃn]	jds Aufmerksamkeit erregen, jdn auf sich aufmerksam machen	to convey [kən'veɪ]	vermitteln, klar machen
		counter ['kaʊntə]	Theke
attitude ['ætɪtjuːd]	Einstellung, Haltung	craic (irisches Wort) [kræk]	Spaß
award-winning [ə'wɔːd ˌwɪnɪŋ]	preisgekrönt	to create suspense [kriˌeɪt sə'spens]	Spannung erzeugen
awareness [ə'weənəs]	Bewusstsein	cuisine [kwɪ'ziːn]	Küche, Kochkunst
awkward ['ɔːkwəd]	peinlich, betreten	current ['kʌrənt]	augenblicklich, gegenwärtig, aktuell

B
back problem ['bæk ˌprɒbləm]	Rückenproblem		
backbone ['bækbəʊn]	Rückgrat	**D** to damage ['dæmɪdʒ]	schaden, beschädigen
based in, to be ~ [bi 'beɪst ɪn]	seinen (Firmen-)Sitz haben in	deadline ['dedlaɪn]	Termin, Frist
		degree [dɪ'griː]	Grad
to behave [bɪ'heɪv]	sich verhalten, sich benehmen	delay [dɪ'leɪ]	Verzögerung
		delicious, to be ~ [bi dɪ'lɪʃəs]	köstlich, lecker sein
to benefit ['benɪfɪt]	nützen, zugute kommen	delighted, to be ~ [bi dɪ'laɪtɪd]	(sehr) erfreut sein
boardroom ['bɔːdruːm]	Sitzungssaal		
to break the ice [ˌbreɪk ði 'aɪs]	das Eis brechen	department [dɪ'pɑːtmənt]	Abteilung
		descent, to be of Turkish ~ [bi əv ˌtɜːkɪʃ dɪ'sent]	türkischer Abstammung sein
brewery ['bruːəri]	Brauerei		
briefcase ['briːfkeɪs]	Aktentasche, -koffer	to destroy [dɪ'strɔɪ]	zerstören
business, to get down to ~ [getˌdaʊn tə 'bɪznəs]	zur Sache kommen	difference, to make all the ~ [ˌmeɪk ɔːl ðə 'dɪfrəns]	viel ausmachen, die Sache völlig verändern
C to catch sth (that has been said) [kætʃ]	(etw Gesagtes) mitbekommen, hören, verstehen	dish [dɪʃ]	Gericht, Speise
		drizzling, It's ~. [ɪts 'drɪzlɪŋ]	Es nieselt.
to cater for ['keɪtə fə]	hier: auf jdn/etw eingestellt sein	to drop sb off [ˌdrɒp 'ɒf]	jdn absetzen
		dump [dʌmp]	hier: Bruchbude, Saustall
charge of, to be in ~ [bi ɪn 'tʃɑːdʒ əv]	verantwortlich sein für	dumpling ['dʌmplɪŋ]	Knödel
		E Easier said than done. [ˌiːziə ˌsed ðən 'dʌn]	Leichter gesagt als getan.
to chat [tʃæt]	plaudern, sich unterhalten		
		embarrassed, to be ~ [bi ɪm'bærəst]	sich genieren, verlegen sein
chef [ʃef]	Küchenchef/in, Chefkoch/köchin		
		embarrassing [ɪm'bærəsɪŋ]	peinlich
chess, to play ~ [ˌpleɪ 'tʃes]	Schach spielen	to emphasize ['emfəsaɪz]	betonen, hervorheben
chit-chat, to make ~ [meɪk 'tʃɪt tʃæt]	plaudern, sich zwanglos unterhalten	employee [ɪm'plɔɪiː]	Angestellte/r, Beschäftigte/r
clarification [ˌklærɪfɪ'keɪʃn]	Klärung, Klarstellung, Erläuterung	to enjoy [ɪn'dʒɔɪ]	genießen, gefallen, gern haben/tun
to close a business deal [ˌkləʊz ə 'bɪznəs diːl]	ein Geschäft abschließen, zum Schluss bringen	enjoyable [ɪn'dʒɔɪəbl]	angenehm
		enormous [ɪ'nɔːməs]	riesig, groß
coal mining ['kəʊlˌmaɪnɪŋ]	(Kohle-)Bergbau	to entertain [ˌentə'teɪn]	unterhalten, (jdn) zu Gast haben
coincidence [kəʊ'ɪnsɪdəns]	Zufall		

	eventually [ɪˈventʃuəli]	schließlich
	exception [ɪkˈsepʃn]	Ausnahme
	exhausted, to be ~ [bi ɪgˈzɔːstɪd]	erschöpft sein
	exhibit [ɪgˈzɪbɪt]	Exponat
	exhibition [ˌeksɪˈbɪʃn]	Ausstellung
	experience [ɪkˈspɪəriəns]	Erfahrung, Erlebnis
F	face, to put a name to a ~ [pʊt ə ˌneɪm tu ə ˈfeɪs]	jdn persönlich kennen lernen, ein Gesicht mit einem Namen versehen
	fact, as a matter of ~ [əz ə ˌmætər əv ˈfækt]	eigentlich, sogar, tatsächlich
	family tree [ˌfæməli ˈtriː]	(Familien-)Stammbaum
	fancy dress [ˌfænsi ˈdres]	Verkleidung, Kostüm
	file [faɪl]	Datei, Papier, Dokument
	to finish sth up [ˌfɪnɪʃ ˈʌp]	aufessen, leer machen
	forthcoming [ˌfɔːθˈkʌmɪŋ]	bevorstehend
	to found [faʊnd]	gründen
	freezing, It's ~. [ɪts ˈfriːzɪŋ]	Es ist sehr kalt.
G	genuinely [ˈdʒenjuɪnli]	echt, wirklich
	to graduate [ˈɡrædʒueɪt]	einen (Hochschul-)Abschluss machen
	to greet sb [ɡriːt]	jdn (be)grüßen
	to grow up [ˌɡrəʊ ˈʌp]	aufwachsen
	grower [ˈɡrəʊə]	Bauer, Züchter
	gym (gymnasium) [dʒɪm, dʒɪmˈneɪziəm]	Sporthalle, Fitness-Studio
H	harbour [ˈhɑːbə]	Hafen
	hay, to be ready to hit the ~ [bi redi tə hɪt ðə ˈheɪ]	reif sein, in die Falle zu gehen
	hazy, It's ~. [ɪts ˈheɪzi]	Es ist diesig/trüb.
	head of, to be ~ [bi ˈhed əv]	(Abteilungs)Leiter/in sein von
	Help yourself. [ˌhelp jɔːˈself]	Bedienen Sie sich.
	herbs [hɜːbz]	Kräuter
	Here you are. [hɪə ju ˈɑː]	Bitte schön (beim Geben).
	host [həʊst]	Gastgeber/in
	huge [hjuːdʒ]	riesig
	humid, It's ~. [ɪts ˈhjuːmɪd]	Es ist feucht.
I	impolite [ˌɪmpəˈlaɪt]	unhöflich
	impressed, to be ~ [bi ɪmˈprest]	beeindruckt sein
	impression [ɪmˈpreʃn]	Eindruck
	to improve [ɪmˈpruːv]	sich verbessern, besser werden
	ingredient [ɪnˈɡriːdiənt]	Zutat (beim Kochen, Backen)
	to introduce sb [ˌɪntrəˈdjuːs]	jdn vorstellen, jdn bekannt machen
J	to join sb [dʒɔɪn]	sich jdm anschließen, mit jdm mitgehen, jdn begleiten
K	to keep going [kiːp ˈɡəʊɪŋ]	am Laufen halten; weitermachen, fortführen
	kitty-corner (AE) [ˈkɪti kɔːnə]	schräg gegenüber
L	lane [leɪn]	Spur, Fahrbahn
	let alone [let əˈləʊn]	geschweige denn
	to look forward to + ing [ˌlʊk ˈfɔːwəd tə]	sich freuen auf
	lunch, to grab a spot of ~ [ˌɡræb ə spɒt əv ˈlʌntʃ]	eine Kleinigkeit zu Mittag essen
M	main course [ˌmeɪn ˈkɔːs]	Hauptgericht
	to make the connection [ˌmeɪk ðə kəˈnekʃn]	die Verbindung herstellen
	to manufacture [ˌmænjuˈfæktʃə]	herstellen, produzieren
	marital status [ˌmærɪtl ˈsteɪtəs]	Familienstand
	matter, for that ~ [fə ˈðæt mætə]	eigentlich, in der Tat
	menu [ˈmenjuː]	Speisekarte
	to mind [maɪnd]	etw dagegen haben
	mouth, you're making my ~ water [jʊə(r) ˌmeɪkːŋ maɪ ˈmaʊθ wɔːtə]	da läuft mir das Wasser im Mund zusammen
	mutual [ˈmjuːtʃuəl]	gegenseitig, gemeinsam
	mutual acquaintance [ˌmjuːtʃuəl əˈkweɪntəns]	gemeinsame/r Bekannte/r
N	to network [ˈnetwɜːk]	(berufliche) Kontakte knüpfen
	nightmare [ˈnaɪtmeə]	Alptraum
	to nip to [ˈnɪp tə]	flitzen zu
O	obliged, to feel ~ [fiːl əˈblaɪdʒd]	sich verpflichtet fühlen
	obsessed, to be ~ [bi əbˈsest]	besessen sein
	occasion [əˈkeɪʒn]	Anlass, Gelegenheit
	offensive [əˈfensɪv]	beleidigend, kränkend
	only child [ˌəʊnli ˈtʃaɪld]	Einzelkind
	to operate [ˈɒpəreɪt]	bedienen; (sich) betätigen
	origin [ˈɒrɪdʒɪn]	Ursprung, Herkunft
	overcast, It's ~. [ɪts ˌəʊvəˈkɑːst]	Es ist bewölkt/hat sich zugezogen.
P	participant [pɑːˈtɪsɪpənt]	Teilnehmer/in
	to pay attention to [peɪ əˈtenʃn tə]	achten auf
	person, to be a small town ~ [bi ə ˌsmɔːl taʊn ˈpɜːsn]	jd sein, der sich in der Kleinstadt wohl fühlt
	pet [pet]	Haustier
	pitcher (of beer) [ˈpɪtʃər]	(Bier-)Krug
	pity, it's a ~ [ɪts ə ˈpɪti]	(es ist) schade
	pleasure [ˈpleʒə]	Vergnügen, Freude
	to pop by [ˌpɒp ˈbaɪ]	vorbeigehen, -schauen
	pouring, It's ~. [ɪts ˈpɔːrɪŋ]	Es regnet in Strömen.
	powerful [ˈpaʊəfl]	stark, überzeugend
	previous [ˈpriːviəs]	vorhergehend, vorherig, früher
	promoted, to get ~ [ɡet prəˈməʊtɪd]	befördert werden
	proposal [prəˈpəʊzl]	Vorschlag
R	to read between the lines [riːd bɪˌtwiːn ðə ˈlaɪnz]	zwischen den Zeilen lesen
	recently [ˈriːsntli]	neulich, vor kurzem, in letzter Zeit
	recommendation [ˌrekəmenˈdeɪʃn]	Empfehlung
	to refer to [rɪˈfɜː tə]	*hier:* sprechen von

to **reply** [rɪˈplaɪ]	antworten	
to **require** [rɪˈkwaɪə]	erfordern, verlangen	
to **restructure** [ˌriːˈstrʌktʃə]	umstrukturieren, umbauen	
to **return a favour** [rɪˌtɜːn ə ˈfeɪvə]	ebenfalls einen Gefallen tun	
reunification [ˌriːjuːnɪfɪˈkeɪʃn]	Wiedervereinigung	
rich [rɪtʃ]	*hier:* reichhaltig	
ring road [ˈrɪŋ rəʊd]	Umgehungsstraße	
roasting, It's ~. [ɪts ˈrəʊstɪŋ]	Es ist glühend heiß.	
rocket science, it's not ~ [ɪts nɒt ˈrɒkɪt saɪəns]	es ist keine Wissenschaft/nicht schwierig	
round the corner [ˌraʊnd ðə ˈkɔːnə]	um die Ecke	
to **round up** [ˌraʊnd ˈʌp]	aufrunden	
rude, to be ~ [bi ˈruːd]	unhöflich sein	
run-down [ˌrʌn ˈdaʊn]	heruntergekommen	

S

satisfied, to feel ~ [fiːl ˈsætɪsfaɪd]	zufrieden sein
savoury [ˈseɪvəri]	herzhaft
self-deprecating [ˌselfˈdeprəkeɪtɪŋ]	selbstironisch, sich selbst auf die Schippe nehmend
sensitive [ˈsensətɪv]	heikel, sensibel
separated, to be ~ [bi ˈsepəreɪtɪd]	getrennt leben/sein
side, to be a bit on the small ~ [bi ə ˌbɪt ɒn ðə ˈsmɔːl saɪd]	vielleicht ein wenig klein sein
side, on the IT ~ of the project [ɒn ði aɪ ˌtiː saɪd əv ðə ˈprɒdʒekt]	bei/für IT-Fragen des Projekts
skill [skɪl]	Fähigkeit, Fertigkeit
slide [slaɪd]	Rutsche
to **solve** [sɒlv]	lösen
sophisticated [səˈfɪstɪkeɪtɪd]	raffiniert, anspruchsvoll
sparkling [ˈspɑːklɪŋ]	mit Kohlensäure
spices [ˈspaɪsɪz]	Gewürze
spicy [ˈspaɪsi]	stark gewürzt, scharf
starter (BE) [ˈstɑːtə]	Vorspeise
step-son [ˈstepsʌn]	Stiefsohn
to **stick to sth** [ˈstɪk tə]	an etw festkleben
straight ahead [ˌstreɪt əˈhed]	geradeaus
to **strike up a conversation** [straɪk ˌʌp ə kɒnvəˈseɪʃn]	ein Gespräch anfangen/beginnen
stuck, to be ~ [bi ˈstʌk]	feststecken
stuffed, to be ~ [bi ˈstʌft]	pappsatt sein
subsidiary [səbˈsɪdiəri]	Tochter(gesellschaft)
successful [səkˈsesfl]	erfolgreich
to **suggest** [səˈdʒest]	vorschlagen

superficial [ˌsuːpəˈfɪʃl]	oberflächlich
supplier [səˈplaɪə]	Lieferant/in, Zulieferer
to **suppose** [səˈpəʊz]	glauben, annehmen
supposed to, to be ~ [bi səˈpəʊzd tə]	sollen, etw tun sollen

T

table service [ˈteɪbl sɜːvɪs]	Bedienung (am Platz)
to **take sb round** [ˌteɪk ˈraʊnd]	*hier:* jdn mitnehmen, jdn herumführen
talking of which [tɔːkɪŋ əv wɪtʃ]	à propos, da/weil wir gerade davon sprechen
tap, on ~ [ɒn ˈtæp]	(Bier) vom Faß
tasty, this is ~ [ðɪs ɪz ˈteɪsti]	das schmeckt sehr gut
taxi rank [ˈtæksi ræŋk]	Taxistand
to **tip** [tɪp]	Trinkgeld geben
touch, to get in ~ [get ɪn ˈtʌtʃ]	(sich) in Verbindung setzen
to **trade** [treɪd]	Handel treiben, handeln
trade fair [ˈtreɪd feə]	Handelsmesse
trust [trʌst]	Vertrauen
to **turn down an invitation** [tɜːn ˌdaʊn ən ɪnvɪˈteɪʃn]	eine Einladung ablehnen

U

ugly [ˈʌgli]	hässlich
unless [ənˈles]	es sei denn

V

venison [ˈvenɪsn]	Hirsch
vocational school [vəʊˌkeɪʃənl ˈskuːl]	Berufsschule; Schule, auf der man einen Beruf erlernen/Berufsabschluss machen kann

W

weather, to be under the ~ [bi ˌʌndə ðə ˈweðə]	nicht recht auf dem Posten/krank sein
weird, to be ~ [bi ˈwɪəd]	merkwürdig, seltsam sein
to **welcome** [ˈwelkəm]	begrüßen, willkommen heißen
wheat beer [ˈwiːt bɪə]	Weizenbier
while you're at it, ... [ˌwaɪl jʊər ˈæt ɪt]	Wenn Sie schon mal dabei sind, ...
work experience [ˈwɜːk ɪkspɪəriəns]	Praktikum, Arbeitserfahrung
to **work out** [ˌwɜːk ˈaʊt]	*hier:* gut laufen
worry [ˈwʌri]	Sorge
worth + *ing*, **to be ~** [bi ˈwɜːθ]	sich lohnen etw zu tun

Y

You're welcome. [jɔː ˈwelkəm]	Bitte schön. (Antwort/Reaktion auf Danke), Keine Ursache!, Gern geschehen.

Useful phrases and vocabulary

MEETING SOMEONE ON ARRIVAL

Greeting a visitor
Hello, I'm Karla Metz from BTO Systems.
You must be Jürgen. Welcome to Berlin.
Nice/Good to see you again. *(when you know sb already)*
– Good to see you too.
It's a pleasure to meet you (at last)./It's great to finally meet you in person. *(meeting sb for the first time)*
– It's a pleasure/Nice/Good/Great to meet you too.
Please, call me Geoff.
– And I'm Lothar, of course.

Apologizing for a delay
I hope you haven't been waiting long.
– Don't worry. I just got here ten minutes ago.
Sorry to keep you waiting. The train was on time but the traffic here is terrible.
– No problem. I know how it is.
Sorry I'm late. My flight was delayed because of bad weather.

Asking about the journey
How was the/your flight/journey/drive?
– Uneventful, thankfully./Fine, thanks.
– Not so good. The traffic was terrible.
– OK, but there was some turbulence.
You must be exhausted now.
– Oh, I'm OK. I managed to get some sleep, actually.
– I am a bit tired, I have to say.

Offering and accepting help
Can I help you with your bags?/Do you need a hand/any help with that?/Shall I take that for you?
– That would be great/very nice, thanks.
Would you mind taking this?
– Not at all./Of course not.
Let me get that for you.

Freshening up
I'd just like to wash my hands (if that's OK/before we get going).
Is there a toilet (BE)/bathroom/restroom (AE) around here/somewhere?
– Yes, there's one just this way ...
Is there a café where we could sit down/get something to drink?
– Yes, there's a nice one just over there.
– I'm not sure, but let's see if we can find one.
Do you mind if we grab/get a quick coffee before we get going?
– Not at all.
– Actually we're in a little bit of a hurry. Maybe we could have one later?

Taking the visitor to their hotel or the company
So, if you'll just come this way ...
The/My car is parked over here.
We can get a taxi over there.
Where are we going from here?
– I thought we could go to the hotel first.
– We should probably go straight to the office, if that's OK.
– I'll take you to your hotel.
Is the hotel/office/conference centre far from here?
– No, it's just 15 minutes away.
– It's probably about a 30-minute drive, but we have plenty of time.

Talking about plans and schedules
It's not far now./We'll be there in five minutes.
I thought you might like to check into your hotel first and drop off your things.
– Sounds good./Sure.
Would you like to check into your hotel first?
– Actually, we can go straight to the office if you prefer.
Then we can grab/get a spot of lunch.
There's a nice Italian place near your hotel.
After that we can go to the company.
We have the meeting with the sales team at 2, as you know.
At 4 we're going to visit the production plant.
That should only take an hour.
Then I'll take you back to your hotel and you can relax for a bit.
I'll pick you up at about 7 for dinner.
We're going to a very nice restaurant this evening.
– Sounds good./Great.

LOOKING AFTER A VISITOR TO YOUR COMPANY

Welcoming a visitor
Hello, Mr Bacon. I'm Lothar Jensburg.
Nice to meet you/see you again.
Welcome to Vierling Design/our company.
Did you have any trouble finding us?
– No, not at all. The directions on your website/Your directions were very clear/good.
Was the driver there to meet you at the airport?
– Yes, he/she was. Thanks so much for arranging that.
– It's the least I could do (after your long flight).
Thanks for coming down to meet me.
– No problem at all. I wasn't sure you'd be able to find my office by yourself.

Showing a visitor around your offices
You can leave your things/your briefcase/coat here/in my office/at the reception desk.
Would you like to leave your things here?
– That would be nice, thanks.

I'll just leave my bag here, if that's OK with you.
I'll take you round to meet a few members of the team.
They're all looking forward to meeting you.
Would you mind waiting in my office for a few minutes?
— Not at all./Sure, no problem.
I just need to make some copies before the meeting.
I thought maybe I could just pop by Roger's office and say hello.
Can/Could I use your bathroom (AE)?
— Of course. I'll just show you where it is.
If you'll just come this way …
Here's the lift now.
After you. *(when entering a lift or going through a door)*

Offering a guest something to eat or drink
Would you like something to drink? Tea, coffee, water…?
So, can I get you something to drink?
— A cup of coffee would be great.
— Just a glass of water, thanks.
— I'm OK for the moment, thanks.
Can I get you a coffee?/How about a cup of tea?
— That would be great/wonderful. Thanks very much.
How do you take your coffee?/How would you like that?
— Just black, thanks.
— With milk/cream (AE), please.
— Milk and sugar, please.
Could I have a glass of water as well, please?
— Coming right up./Of course.
Here you are./Here's your coffee. *(giving a drink)*
Thank you.
— You're welcome./No problem.
— Not at all./Don't mention it.
Shall we get some lunch?
— Sounds good. It's been a long time since breakfast.
— Maybe I'll just have a coffee. I'm not actually that hungry.

Giving directions
Where are you now?/Where is your office now?
— On the fourth floor./Just down here.
Which floor is your office on?
— The eighth! Don't worry – we'll take the lift/elevator (AE).
Where is the toilet/bathroom (AE)/Mike's office?
It's just down the hall/round the corner on the left/right.
It's the first/second/third door on the left/right.
It's next to the toilet/front door/kitchen.
Just go out of the door and turn left to get to the lift.
— That's very clear, thanks./Thanks, I'm sure I'll find it.
— Sorry, could you explain that again?
Come with me and I'll show you where it is!
I'll meet you back here in ten minutes, OK?
— Sounds good. See you soon!

Introducing a visitor to your colleagues
The first person I'd like you to meet is Verena Fellstein.
She's our marketing manager.
Verena, this is Geoff Bacon.
— It's a pleasure to meet you, Geoff./It's great to finally meet you.

— Nice to meet you too.
And this is Marion Tischler, our product designer.
I'd like to introduce Mr Bacon. He's the new head of production.
Have the two of you met before?
— No, we haven't, but we've exchanged a lot of emails.
— Yes, (I think) we actually met once at a trade fair.
It's nice to put a name to a face, isn't it?
— It certainly is.
I think you've had contact with her.
She'll be your contact person on the IT side of the project.
You'll have a chance to get to know everyone a bit better at this afternoon's meeting.
I'm afraid I'm not very good with names.
— I know what you mean!

At a meeting
Sorry, it always takes a few minutes for everyone to arrive.
— Not to worry./No problem.
Hi, everyone, sorry I'm a bit late. I just needed to gather some files for our meeting.
So, if everyone would like to take a copy of today's agenda …
Well, I suppose we should make a start.
So, shall we get down to business?
Right, let's make a start, shall we?
So, shall we start again at, say, 3.30? *(before a break)*
— Sounds good.

ENTERTAINING A VISITOR

Showing a visitor around your town or city
This is the old town square/cathedral (here).
Let me show you the museum/town hall.
This kind of architecture is typical of our region.
That's the castle I was telling you about earlier.
It was built/designed by …
It's really impressive/beautiful.
I've never seen a building like this before.
How old is it?
— I think it's from the 15th century but I'm not totally sure.

Asking for/Giving recommendations for sightseeing
I've actually got the afternoon free tomorrow.
I was wondering if you had any recommendations for things to do.
I know what you can do.
There's a(n) great/fantastic/interesting art gallery/shop/park/street.
There's a nice exhibition of photos on at the town hall at the moment.
There's a fantastic coal mining museum just an hour from here.
If we have time we can maybe show you one of the lakes nearby.
— That would be nice./Sounds great.
It's/They're very interesting/beautiful/amazing.

I can take you if you like.
It's really/definitely worth visiting/seeing/a visit.
I'd really like to do that./I'd love to see that.

Asking for/Giving directions in a town or city
Where is the town hall/station/museum exactly?
How do I get there?/What's the best way to get there?
It's next to/near/just around the corner from/on the same street as your hotel/the town hall/square.
Just go along this street, then turn left/right.
Take the second/third street on the left/right.
Keep going until you see the church/bank.
You can walk there from here.

Invitations
Making an invitation
I was wondering if you might like to join us for dinner tonight?
How about meeting for a coffee next week?
I have a spare ticket for the opera tonight. Would you like to come?
My partner and I are having a party next Saturday. We were hoping you could come.

Accepting an invitation
That sounds really nice/great. Thanks very much.
Thanks, I'd like that very much.
That would be lovely.
Good idea. Let's do that.

Turning down an invitation
I'd love to but I'm actually away at a trade fair all next week.
That's very kind of you but I'm supposed to be meeting a friend for dinner this evening.
I'd love to come, but I'm afraid I just don't have time today.

Making an alternative suggestion
How about the week after that?
Maybe you can let me know next time you're going?
Maybe we could go for dinner tomorrow instead?
How about having lunch sometime next week?

EATING OUT

Restaurant small talk
I'm excited about the food.
I have to say it's been a long time since lunch.
I'm a bit hungry/absolutely starving.
Do you come here often?
– Oh yes. I was here last week actually.
– Usually just when I have guests.
I used to come here a lot when I worked in the centre of town.
The portions are pretty enormous here.
You're making my mouth water!
That was delicious but if I eat any more I'm going to explode.

Helping with the menu
I'm afraid they don't have English menus here.
Just say if you need help with anything.
I might need help with some of this.
Is that some kind of meat?
So what's …?
– It's a kind of fish/meat/vegetable/pasta/ dumpling.
– It's (a bit) like an omelette.
– It's made with eggs, milk and sugar.
– It's a(n) Austrian/German/Swiss speciality.
– It's typical of/a speciality of our region.
– It's a spicy/savoury/sweet dish.
– It's made with meat/fish/vegetables.
You have to try that/those.

Ordering
Do you know what you're having?
Have you decided yet?
– Yes. I think I'll have the steak.
– I'm still trying to make up my mind. It all looks so good.
– I think I need a couple more minutes, if that's OK.
(I think) I'll have that for my main course (then).
I'm going to have the cheese 'Spätzle'/the special.
Let's see if we can catch the waiter's attention.
I'd like/I'll have the pasta, please. *(to the waiter)*

Paying for the meal
Shall we get the bill?
I'll see if I can catch the waiter when he goes past.
Can we have the bill, please? *(to the waiter)*
Could you bring us the bill, please?
Let me get this./This is on me./I'll get this.
– No, it's OK. I'll get it.
– Are you sure? That's very kind/generous of you.
That was lovely, thank you./Thanks for the meal. It was really nice.
– You're very welcome.
– It was my/a pleasure.
What do I do about tipping?
– You just round up the total.
– I normally leave … per cent.
I don't have any cash on me.
Do they accept credit cards here?

AT A TRADE FAIR

Starting a conversation with a stranger
I'm sorry, but I couldn't help noticing you've got a Chipper bag. Do you work for them?
Excuse me, do you know if this is the stop for the trade fair?
Excuse me, do you mind if I join you?
– Not at all.
Are you here for the trade fair?
– Yes, exactly.
I'm Ute Adena, by the way.
– Lloyd Roberts. Nice to meet you.

Talking about the trade fair
Are you looking after a stand at the fair?
– Yes, we have a stand here.
– I'm actually just here to look around and do some networking.
When did you get here?
– On Wednesday./Just today, actually.
So, what do you think of the fair so far?
– I'm enjoying it a lot.
– It's quite good. Certainly better than last year.
– I'm a bit disappointed, to tell the truth.
Have you seen anything interesting?
– Yes, one company has developed a really nice .../some interesting new ...
– Not really, to be honest.
That sounds like something worth checking out.
If you want to take a look, just go to section/hall B.
The stand is right near the door.
Thanks for the tip!

Talking about your company
What company are you with?
– I'm the head of purchasing at Pixdorf.
– I'm with a French company called Plein Air.
And what about you? What do you do?
And who do you work for?
What does your company do (exactly)?
– We make software for retail POS systems.
I've heard of your company before. Where are you based?
– In Toulouse. Do you know it?
Am I right in thinking you're based in Frankfurt?
– Yes, that's right.
– Well, just outside Frankfurt actually.

Talking to a person at a stand
So you see we really have some very exciting new products/services.
It's really one of our most interesting developments.
I absolutely have to show you/demonstrate our new ...
It'll only take a minute.
It's/They're certainly very interesting.

Ending a conversation
Anyway, let me give you my card.
Listen, do you have a card?
Why don't I come back afterwards to take a look?
Sorry, I really have to go now.
I should really get going. I have another appointment in a couple of minutes.
I'm actually supposed to be meeting someone in ten minutes.
Listen, I've just seen Chris over there. Excuse me a moment, I really need to catch him.

MISCELLANEOUS COMMUNICATION SKILLS

Reacting to what someone says
That must be very stressful/an interesting job.
You must be very proud of her.
That must have been very exciting/nice.
That must have been a difficult time for you.

Asking for clarification
(I'm) sorry, I didn't quite catch that.
(I'm) sorry, could you tell me your name again?
Sorry, could you say that for me again?
I'm sorry, I don't quite follow you.
I'm not totally sure what you mean.
Did you say 15 or 50?

Keeping a conversation going
Have you ever been to Hong Kong?
– No, I haven't. What about you?
– Yes, I have. I was there two years ago on business.
This is actually my second visit.
– Oh really? When were you here before?

SMALL TALK

Talking about the weather
How was the weather when you left?
– It was raining, as usual!/It was very nice, actually.
I can't believe it's so sunny/hot/cold here.
What a beautiful day!
– It is, isn't it?
It was actually snowing when I left home.
This summer/winter has been terrible/OK/lovely/great.
The last couple of weeks have been very warm/cold.
Do you normally get good summers here?
– Usually we get at least a few hot days, but sometimes it rains a lot.
– Not really!
I imagine the winters here must be pretty cold.
– Oh yes. Sometimes it goes down to minus 15.
– Actually they're not as cold as you might think.

Talking about travel
Is this your first time in Germany?
– Actually, no, I've been here a few times.
– Actually, I was here once before, in 2001.
– Yes it is. I'm really enjoying it.
Have you been here before?
– No, this is my first time.
– Yes, I've been here a couple of times.
When were you here before?
– I was here two years ago/in 2005.
Have you ever been to England?
– Just once, when I was a teenager. I did a school exchange to London.
– No, never. I've always wanted to go there.
Was that for business or pleasure?
– It was a business trip.
– I was just there on holiday. It was very relaxing!
– A bit of both.
Did you enjoy your visit to ...?

– Yes, very much. Especially the food!
– It was OK, but the weather wasn't so great.
What did you think of …?
– It's an amazing city. Pity about the weather though!
Where did you stay when you were there?
– We found this fantastic hotel right next to the river.

Talking about a company's offices
This is a lovely space you have here.
It's a really nice building – very bright and airy.
It's a huge improvement on our previous building.
To be honest, I liked the old building better.
It's a great neighbourhood – lots of green space and some nice cafés.
The only problem is there are no restaurants nearby/it's difficult to park here.
Have you been in this location long?
– No, we actually just moved into this building six months ago.
– Yes, we've been here for more than ten years.

Talking about a company
How long has your company been around?
– It was founded by Detlef Vierling ten years ago.
– We've been going for almost 50 years.
How many people are in the company now?
– We currently have 31 employees.
– We have about 200 staff at the moment.
We've really expanded over the last few years.

Talking about mutual acquaintances
How's Marita these days?
What's Carol up to?
Have you heard anything from Josef recently?
What about Chris? How's he doing these days?
– He's doing fine.
Is Anja still with the company, by the way?
– She's not, actually. She left last July.
– Yes, she's still here.
As a matter of fact she's in Bristol now.
Do you know what she's doing there?
I heard from him/her a couple of weeks ago.
He/She was promoted to product manager recently.
Is that Chris Bennett you're talking about?
– Exactly.
He/She says hello, by the way.
I should send him/her an email.
Say hi to Maria for me. *(informal)*
Give my regards to Maria. *(neutral/formal)*
Should I tell him/her hi from you?
– Could you? That would be nice.

Talking about personal possessions
That's an interesting painting/picture/photograph you've got there.
I like that painting/picture/photograph. Where did you get it?
It's very colourful/beautiful/interesting/different.
I couldn't help noticing your new Palm Pilot.

Talking about where you are from
Are you from Schwarzburg originally?
– Yes, I am.
– No, I'm actually from Dresden.
I'm actually from a little village just outside Stuttgart.
I was born in Vienna, but I grew up in Graz.
I used to live in Schweinfurt.
I went to university in Greifswald.
I graduated from university in 1995.
Where did you live before that?
Did you go to college/university/vocational school in [name of town/city]?
What did you study?
Do you ever miss America?
– Yes, I do. Especially the food!
– Not really, but I do miss my family.
– Not at all! I'm very happy here.

Talking about where you live
I live in/near/not far from …
How long have you lived here?
Do you like living here?
It's maybe a bit on the small side.
The cultural life is really good.
There's a lot going on.
It's quite expensive to live here.
It's really nice that you can be out in the countryside in just thirty minutes.

Talking about free-time activities
So, what do you like doing in your free time?
Do you have any hobbies?/Do you do any sports?
I love/like/don't like/hate cooking/reading.
I often go to the gym/play tennis/do yoga after work/at the weekend.
I like swimming/sailing/going to the theatre but I never have the time.
I try to play football/squash at least once a week.
If I had more time, I would go to more concerts/eat out more.

Talking about family relationships
Are you married (as well)?
– Yes, I just got married last year, actually.
– No, I live with my partner.
– I'm actually single at the moment.
Let me show you some photos.
Do you have any brothers or sisters?
Is [name] married?
Does [name] have any children?
How old is [name]?
[Name] got married in 2002.
He/She has … children.
They are married/separated/divorced.
He/She is … years old.
My husband/wife is a meteorologist/an analyst.
My son/daughter has just got a place at university.

Vocabulary banks

THE WEATHER

words describing weather in general	words describing temperature	words describing the sky	words to do with water	weather verbs
good	freezing	cloudy	wet	to rain
great	cold	grey	damp	to pour
fantastic	chilly	overcast	drizzling	to drizzle
lovely	mild	clear	humid	to freeze
OK	warm	sunny	pouring	to hail
changeable	hot		rainy	to snow
depressing	boiling			to shine
miserable	roasting			to cloud over/to clear up (sky)
terrible				

COMPANIES

talking about the building	talking about the company structure	verbs to do with the history of the company or building	adjectives for rooms and buildings
location	employees	to found	bright
(first/second/third) floor	staff	to set up	sunny
reception (area)	personnel	to expand	airy
lift/elevator (AE)	colleagues	to open a new office	light
stairs	department	to close an office/a department	dark
neighbourhood	division	to restructure	crowded
toilet/bathroom/restroom (AE)	branch	to downsize	spacious
kitchen	subsidiary	to move (into/out of)	old
photocopier room	parent company	to take on new staff	modern
meeting/conference room	head office	to lay off staff	beautiful
car park	hierarchy		ugly

types of furniture and office equipment	company departments
(office) chair	administration
stool	bookkeeping/accounts
table	purchasing
desk	sales & marketing
reception desk	production
cupboard	legal
notice board	research & development (R&D)
whiteboard	logistics
flipchart	customer services
overhead projector	technical support
data projector	IT

FREE-TIME ACTIVITIES

sport	relaxing at home	going out	Hobbies and pastimes
playing football/squash/tennis/golf	listening to music	eating out/going to restaurants	playing cards/board games
(going) sailing/swimming/skiing/jogging/cycling/inline skating	reading	going to the cinema/theatre/opera/museums/concerts/pubs/bars	doing crosswords/puzzles/Sudoku
keeping fit	watching television	(going) shopping	photography/drawing/painting
going to the gym	cooking	going clubbing	DIY/home improvements
doing yoga/karate/tai chi	visiting friends	meeting friends	
	doing nothing		

Vocabulary banks | 84

TOWNS AND CITIES

places in a town/city

airport
harbour
railway station
bus station
art gallery
museum
castle
cathedral
mosque
synagogue
park
sports/leisure centre
swimming pool
old town centre
town/city hall
shopping centre/mall (AE)
university

words to describe towns/cities

beautiful
historic
important
industrial
thriving
fashionable
growing
large
small
ancient
old
modern
cheap
expensive

phrases to describe relative size and location

a bit bigger than
much smaller than
about the same size as
(not that) close to
near
right next to
part of
on the (name of river)

FOOD

parts of the meal

aperitif
starter
main course
dessert/pudding (BE)
digestif

types of meat

bacon
beef
chicken
ham
lamb
pork
rabbit
veal
venison

types of vegetable

aubergine/ eggplant (AE)
pepper
(red) cabbage
courgette (BE)/ zucchini (AE)
onion
cucumber
lettuce
sweetcorn
mushroom
turnip
parsnip

side dishes

chips (BE)/ French fries (AE)
potato wedges
rice
salad
noodles

ways of cooking

to bake
to fry
to deep fry
to grill (BE)/to broil (AE)
to roast
to toast
to sauté
to microwave

describing food

heavy
light
rich
savoury
spicy
sweet
fatty
fattening
salty
sugary
tasty
delicious
disgusting

dairy products

milk
cheese
yoghurt
cream cheese

describing hunger

hungry
peckish
starving
ravenous
full
stuffed

FAMILY AND RELATIONSHIPS

words to describe marital status

single
engaged
married
separated
divorced
widowed

words for talking about family members and friends

mother-in-law
father-in-law
brother-in-law
sister-in-law
step-daughter
step-son
only child
ex-wife
ex-husband
best friend
acquaintance

verbs connected to families and relationships

to be born
to meet someone
to make sb's acquaintance
to introduce sb to sb
to get to know sb
to get engaged
to get married
to separate
to get divorced
to be pregnant
to have a baby